HISTORY OF THE RENAISSANCE
1350–1550

BOOK I
ECONOMY and SOCIETY

by
EMIL LUCKI

University of Utah Press

Table of Contents

Chapter IV

BANKING AND FINANCE 79

Chapter V

THE ROLE OF THE STATE IN THE ECONOMIC LIFE OF THE RENAISSANCE AND ECONOMIC THEORY 100

Chapter VI

RENAISSANCE SOCIETY 121

Editor's Note

D R. EMIL LUCKI'S *History of the Renaissance* is the product of many years of study and teaching in the field and of his conviction that in the past some important phases of Renaissance civilization were not given sufficient emphasis in the general histories of the Renaissance. The result quite naturally turned out to be a thorough and a comprehensive manuscript, but too large to be published at today's costs as a single volume; and since printing it in two volumes was precluded by the organization of the work in five parts, the decision was therefore made to conform to the organization of the manuscript and to print it in five quality, but modestly priced, paperbacks. This latter project is now underway with the present Book I, the second of the series to appear, Book III, *Education, Learning, and Thought,* having been published in September of 1963.

Aside from the obvious virtues of a small and inexpensive book, two other important considerations dictated the decision.

While the series on the Renaissance is labeled "history," the subject matter of each book is of such a nature that the individual books in the series should appeal not only to students of history but also to students in the various other disciplines that are concerned with the study of Western culture. Thus, students of religion should find Book II, *The Church and Religion,* of great use; and students of the humanities, especially those interested in education, philosophy, and science, will discover Book III of equally high value. Book V, *Politics and Political Theory,* may be expected to appeal to political science majors; and majors in the arts and in literature are likely to find much of value in Book IV, *Literature and Art.* Finally, the present book on Economy and Society should be welcome to students of business and economics. Thus, while the series as a whole can be used as a history textbook on the Renaissance, individual books can be used as collateral and enrichment reading in other courses.

Another reason for publishing the manuscript in several volumes is to make it easily available to the general public. The message and the style of the work are of such a nature that the work should be made available to as wide an audience as possible; and publishing it in one expensive volume or even in two would have defeated the purpose — hence the decision to print it in five handy books.

The University of Utah Press is indeed pleased to have a part in publishing Professor Lucki's *History of the Renaissance*. We believe it is a work which both in its entirety and severally through its parts will leave its mark in the academic world and among the reading public at large.

A. R. Mortensen

Preface to the Series

ONE WAY to ascertain the character of a society at a given epoch is to study its economy, religion and church, education and thought, literature and art, and its politics. If the purpose of the inquiry is also to discover in what ways this society differs from that of the preceding age, then a similar examination of the civilization of the earlier period becomes a necessity.

Such are the purposes and nature of this series of five small books on the Renaissance. They will attempt to describe Renaissance civilization and at the same time to discover in what ways this civilization was new and to what extent it was an outgrowth of the Middle Ages.

The purposes of the work naturally determine the chronological limits of the period to be studied. In general, scholars who write about the Renaissance date it approximately from 1350 to 1550. However, while the span of these two centuries may be accepted as the core of the Renaissance period, the dates 1350 and 1550 cannot possibly be regarded as fixed termini. In connection with the history of the church, for example, the date 1517, the year when Luther posted his ninety-five theses, has far more significance as a dividing date than the year 1550. It would be more meaningful, therefore, to stop the survey of church history at 1517 than at 1550. On the other hand, to terminate the survey of astronomy at 1550 would be unjustified, for the Copernican revolution, although made public in 1543, did not gain acceptance until at least a century had elapsed. Similarly, the logical beginning of the study of Renaissance Papacy is not with the events of the year 1350 but with the clash between Boniface VIII and Philip IV of France which occurred some fifty years earlier; and the study of Italian Renaissance painting, not with the works of some painter or painters of the year 1350, but with those of Giotto, whose dates are 1276–1336, or with those of Cimabue who lived even earlier, from about 1240 to 1301. It is clear, therefore, that in any survey of the Renaissance age the beginning and the terminal dates will vary with each aspect of the Renaissance civilization. Dates which may be appropriate for literature may not be appropriate for science, and dates which may hold true for Italy may not apply to Germany.

Aside from the matter of dating the Renaissance, three other factors have influenced the nature and the organization of this work.

One of these additional factors is the secondary purpose of the work, namely, the attempt to discover how the Renaissance civilization was influenced by the preceding age. To answer this crucial question it is necessary to look at the pre-Renaissance century; and so, in general, each phase of the civilization is treated in two stages, the late medieval stage and the Renaissance stage.

A very strong second factor is the desire to provide the reader with an adequate cross-sectional view of each phase of the civilization as well as with its historical, developmental process. If the focus were on the latter alone, then the work would result in a survey of the new developments, in an account, for example, of the growth of a capitalistic economy and not in a picture of the entire economy, or of the decline of the church and not in a view of the church as a whole. Such a treatment would simply reinforce the traditional notion that the Renaissance was a period of innovations, which, while true in part, is certainly in need of revision.

The third factor is the desire to show the several sides to the Renaissance civilization. To accomplish this task, clearly all the major aspects of the civilization need to be examined, and the examination must be comprehensive. Accordingly, some aspects, such as agriculture, economic theory, church organization, educational system, historiography, and diplomacy, are studied at length because to date they have been slighted in histories on the Renaissance; while others, even those which are usually emphasized, such as humanism and art, are treated in considerable detail in order to bring out clearly their dependence on, and deviation from, the medieval civilization.

If this comprehensiveness has resulted, in some places, in a wealth of factual information, the reader is assured that the facts are presented not as ends in themselves, to be learned, but as guides to interpretation. With too few facts at his disposal the reader would have insufficient information upon which to base his judgments, and he would have to depend upon the author's interpretations. While some dependence on the writer is inescapable, it should be reduced to the minimum, as the purpose of any academic discipline is to encourage independence of mind but dependence on evidence. The facts in these books are intended to serve just such a purpose.   EMIL LUCKI

Preface to Book I

IN THE PAST the economy of the Renaissance period has generally been
treated as the function of a rising middle class and of the emergence
of modern capitalism. It is possible, of course, to find evidence of both
these economic developments in the two centuries (1350–1550) covered
by this study. But to base one's interpretation of Renaissance economy
on such evidence alone is to base it on a very limited foundation and
to come up with a one-sided conclusion. To correct this interpretation
is then the purpose of this work.

The economy of any period is the product of the people's principal
economic occupations of that time. Hence, if we wish to understand the
economy of the Renaissance period, we need to study the agriculture,
commerce, industry, and finance of the time, and to examine the contemporary economic thought. This is what is attempted in the several
chapters of this brief work.

What is essayed, however, is not just an account of the changes
which may have developed in these occupations during the Renaissance
period, but also an analysis of their natures, that is, of the ways in which
they were organized and how they operated. Such a dual treatment
is likely to result in a more realistic picture of these occupations and
so of the Renaissance economy in general.

Because one purpose of this book is to ascertain how the Renaissance
and medieval economies differed from each other and how they were
related, frequent allusions are necessarily made to the way things were
done in the medieval period. One can get a truer picture of the Renaissance economy and so of the Renaissance civilization as a whole only if
one keeps a constant eye on the economies of both periods.

Included in this book is a chapter on society. The reason for the
inclusion is obvious: society is determined basically by three factors, by
the way the people make their living, by what they study and know, and
by what they believe. The first book in this series, Book III, *Education,
Learning, and Thought,* examined the second of these factors; this one
explores the first factor; and the forthcoming book, Book II, *The Church
and Religion,* will deal with the church and religion. Logically then,
we might have postponed our examination of the society until the appearance of the next book. However, practical considerations dictated
the inclusion of the chapter on society here, as it is easier, for example,

to lead into the study of the peasant class after one has studied agriculture than after one has studied the parish or the catholic doctrine. Hence the inclusion of the subject of society in this work on economy.

In our study of society, the peasantry is given more attention than is usual in histories on the Renaissance. The emphasis in justifiable as the peasantry constituted the great majority of the population, perhaps upwards of 75 per cent. The emphasis is also deliberate, as it provides a corrective to the customary interpretation of the Renaissance as an era of prosperity and of the rise of the bourgeois class to prominence. The purpose is not to deny the traditional view insofar as the traditional view is correct, but simply to put it in proper perspective, against the somber backdrop, as it were, of the life of the great majority of the people who were neither bourgeois nor prosperous.

EMIL LUCKI

CHAPTER I   *Agriculture and Ranching*

O NE COULD begin the study of Renaissance economy with an examination of commerce and the related business activities. But if
this were done, the impression might be created that commerce was the
most important economic enterprise in those days. This, of course,
would be misleading. For, while commerce, industry, and banking
played a significant role in the way of life of the people during the
Renaissance, agriculture surpassed them all in importance. Hence, if
the proper perspective of the Renaissance economy is to be preserved,
agriculture needs to be given prime consideration.

Agriculture

GRAIN FARMING For the millions of Europeans in the Renaissance
period farming was the basic occupation. There may have been places
in Europe, as Flanders and north-central Italy, where a great number of
people were employed in industry and commerce, perhaps even more
than in agriculture. But except for these few places of industrial concentration, the great majority of the population, anywhere from 75 to
90 per cent, continued to make their living off the land. They plowed,
sowed, reaped, and threshed, and then some of their produce they saved
for food and seed and some they sold for money or bartered for other
commodities and services. To supplement their meager fare and income
they also raised cattle, sheep, hogs, and poultry. This was a simple but
enduring method of making a living, almost as prevalent in the Renaissance period as in the preceding age.

To carry on this vital industry the farmer of the Renaissance days
followed traditional techniques and methods as they came down from
ancient times or as they had been modified by the agricultural and social revolutions in the course of the Middle Ages,[1] with only small
changes. He continued to plow his land twice a year, although north

1

of the Alps three plowings were becoming common. The plow he used was either the wheelless light plow known as the *aratrum* or the heavy-wheeled machine. The first he used on light soils, on small plots, or if that was all he could afford; the second, on heavy soils and on spacious fields. Both plows were centuries old; the *aratrum* apparently remained unchanged; the wheeled plow added a coulter and a moldboard, which, though known and used during the Middle Ages, became standard equipment during the Renaissance period. To crumble the soil of the plowed fields it was customary to drag over it the harrow, a latticed frame with spikes projecting from the intersections. In connection with this operation two changes began to appear. One was the shift from the square to the diamond form of harrow which made the implement easier to draw. The other was the use of horses instead of oxen to pull it, since the speedier gait of horses resulted in more effective harrowing. However, this substitution was not widespread, as the average peasant could not afford horses; nor was it a Renaissance innovation, for notices of the horse being used for harrowing appear as early as the eleventh century — for example, on the Bayeaux tapestry. Sowing remained unchanged, the seed being broadcast by hand. Reaping was done with the age-old sickles and scythes, sickles being used for cutting wheat and rye, and scythes for oats and barley. There are some indications that scythes began to be used for cutting wheat also, presumably to reduce costs of harvesting, since mowing is a speedier process. Threshing was done by beating the grain with a stick or flail, or by having cattle tramp over the dried sheaves on the threshing floor. The wooden rake and the sieve helped separate the grain from the chaff. Finally, the two-wheeled cart, generally ox-drawn, or a pack animal took the grain to the local market or to the water-driven flour mill.

If the farmer of the Renaissance period adopted few significant changes in the techniques of farming, he was not much more progressive in the science of farming. In some places he plowed his land three or four times to clear it of weeds and to pulverize the soil. There are indications also that some farmers in northern Italy, Flanders, Germany, and England had discovered the value of legumes not only as fodder for their stock but also as fertilizers of soil. But these innovations were not widespread. Most of the farmers continued to rehabilitate their land in the traditional ways: they fallowed after every two or three crops; they grazed their cattle on the harvested fields; they spread manure and marl; or they allowed the land to revert to a wild state for several years at a time. Aside from these customary methods they knew no other way of enriching their soil; and for this ignorance they paid a penalty in the meagerness of the harvests they gathered. Mother Earth may have been heavy, but in the period of the Renaissance as in the Middle Ages she was not prolific with seed. Her yield was always grudging and small, seldom more than five or six times the amount of grain seeded.

VITICULTURE While cereal farming and gardening prevailed in most of Europe, there were places where viticulture was almost as important. In Italy, France, Spain, and in parts of Rhenish and south-central Germany the inhabitants used wine as a staple in their diet, and so they utilized much of their arable for growing grapes. Indeed in some parts of these regions grape growing exceeded grain farming; while in others the two were combined in the same fields, grain being raised between the rows of grapevines. It is likely also that viticulture actually expanded during the Renaissance period, if the expansion which has been established for France[2] can be postulated for other north European lands too. The reason for the increase in France appears to have been the spread of the custom of drinking wine from the urban aristocracy to their servants and from the latter to their social equals, namely, the artisan class. This spread attained substantial proportions by the middle of the fourteenth century; and to meet the demands of the new clientele, taverns began to be multiplied and the production of wine to be increased, especially in the vicinity of the larger towns.

But if there was expansion in the industry, there was practically no change in the cultivating operations. In the Garonne Valley, a region where viticulture was the prevailing industry and therefore the most likely place for innovations to occur, the method remained unchanged. The operations began just before the winter season. For new vineyards the soil was prepared late in the fall and the vines planted. In old vineyards, young vines were planted to replace dead ones. Around February the vines were thinned and fastened to their supports. In summer the roots were "covered" and "uncovered" and the sappers and useless foliage were pruned. From the end of August through

October the fruit was gathered, pressed by human feet, fermented in vats, and then barreled for home use and for sale. Naturally there could be no change in these seasonal operations. But — and this is significant — there were no developments in the implements used nor in the science of cultivation. On large estates where the terrain was level the *aratrum* was used to prepare the soil for planting and to cultivate the growing vines, and where retouching was necessary the hoe was employed. On terraced vineyards the hoe alone did the work. The sickle and the pruning knife did the other job. To fertilize the soil, manure was used, or the mash from the vats, or vegetation that was gathered from the Garonne and its tributaries. Finally, most of the vineyards were rented in small patches to peasants who could seldom raise enough capital to finance innovations. All this was age-old and remained unaltered. Recent studies of viticulture in other areas of France agree on this point.[3]

SPECIALIZED CROPS Grain growing and viticulture were the main but not the only forms of agriculture practiced during the Renaissance: there was also some cultivation of specialized crops. Olives, the oil of which was in great demand for food and for the manufacture of dyes, were grown in parts of Italy and Spain; saffron, in demand as a yellow dye and as a condiment, was cultivated in the Abruzzi region of Italy, in Aragon, and in southern France; and woad, from which the popular blue dyes were made, was raised in the vicinity of Toulouse, in Picardy, Silesia, and Thuringia. Hops, needed for beer processing, while known in the Middle Ages, began to be cultivated widely in the Renaissance period. Flax was raised extensively in Hainaut and Naples and converted into linen; and hemp, from whose fibers rope was made, though likely to be found almost anywhere, was grown in great quantities in the territory of Emilia, Italy, but especially in east-central Europe. All of these products were cultivated in the traditional manner.

INNOVATIONS: MARKET GARDENING AND NEW CROPS But all was not tradition. In addition to the several minor changes noted above, two more significant developments began to appear. One was the tendency toward specialization in market gardening and the growing of hops. It was customary for townsmen in the Middle Ages to grow their own vegetables on their own garden plots, but in the last century of the Renaissance period, in more urbanized areas, many farmers began to convert their grainfields into gardens to supply the urban markets with vegetables. The same is true of hops. While north Europeans in general were heavy consumers of beer, it was in the populous cities that the demands were heaviest, and so fields of hops tended to be concentrated close to the market. The other development was the introduction of some new grains, vegetables, and fruits. Buckwheat came with the Mongols and appeared in eastern Germany in the early part of the fifteenth century. Thence it spread westward rapidly, and within a century it was common throughout France. White lettuce and cantaloupe spread northward from Italy in the fifteenth century. Cultivated fruits displaced their wild counterparts, as, for example, the cider apple and the strawberry. Known in the Middle Ages, they came into wide use during the Renaissance period. Finally, maize and tobacco may be included in this list although they came late in the period. Maize reached Europe in the days of Columbus, and within half a century spread throughout the continent. Fuchs, for example, included a description of it in his herbal which appeared in 1542. However, during the Renaissance, it was grown as a curiosity rather than as a cereal. Tobacco was brought to Spain before the end of the Renaissance and to France and England by 1560 and quickly gained the fancy of the Europeans. Taken as a cure at first, it soon was smoked for pleasure. Demand for it rose rapidly, and by the end of the century tobacco farming, again close to the cities, had become a promising agricultural industry.

No Substantial Increase of Arable   If these innovations had been accompanied by an increase in the acreage under cultivation, there might have been a noticeable effect on the economy of the age. But the fact is that there was no such increase in western Europe as a whole.

Historians assure us that the great *défrichement* which began in the eleventh century came to an end in the early 1300's and that thereafter, because of the great drop in population, there was not much breaking of new lands and colonizing in western Europe. Some new lands were wrested in northern and central Italy from the slopes of the Riviera, from the Po, and from the marshes of Lombardy and Tuscany; a small area was recovered from the Zuider Zee which in 1377 and 1421 had flooded some twenty townships; and some additional grain lands were opened between the Vistula and the Niemen. But what was added in the south and along the North and the Baltic seas was more than counterbalanced by the abandonment of arable elsewhere. The Black Plague seriously depleted the labor force, making it necessary for owners of large farms to let parts of their land go uncultivated. Then the devastations, in France because of the Hundred Years' War, in eastern Germany because of the repeated wars between the Teutonic Knights and Poland, in Bohemia because of the Hussite wars, and in Sweden because of the chronic wars against Danish overlordship, forced the abandonment of additional arable. Thus in England, for example, more than 450 villages and hamlets were abandoned, some, no doubt, due to the enclosure movement; and in eastern and southwestern Germany about one-fourth of the farming communities disappeared.[4] Renaissance Europe simply had no renaissance of *défrichement,* and its agricultural output could therefore show no gain.

ORGANIZATIONAL SYSTEM OF FARMING: THE MANORIAL SYSTEM If changes in the agricultural operations were not significant, changes in the organization of the farming system were substantial. But the reader should be warned in advance not to assume that these changes, however important they may have been in some aspects, had a commensurate impact on the agricultural economy or on the Renaissance economy as a whole.

At the beginning of the Renaissance period the prevailing organization in agriculture was still the medieval manorial system. To be sure, there were some regions in western Europe without the manorial system. Tuscany and some parts of northern Italy, for example, did not have it, perhaps because money was more readily available there than in northern Europe and so the landlords did not need serfs to cultivate the demesne lands.[5] In southwestern France, in the foothills of Spain, and in Switzerland the terrain did not lend itself to large-estate farming and so to manorialism. And in scattered sections of northern and western England the persisting land customs of the Celts and Danes as well as the ruggedness of the terrain impeded the development of organized manorialism. But in the rest of Europe the manorial system was common, almost universal.

The manor was a large estate consisting normally of five parts: the manor yard with the manor house and the other requisite buildings, including the mill, the oven, and, where grapes were grown, the wine press; the village community; the arable; the woods whence came the fuel and timber and where the pigs grubbed for food; and the meadow, the source of pasture and of hay for the cattle of the villagers and the manor lord.

The arable was normally divided into three large fields to permit the triennial plan of crop rotation. Each of these fields was in turn divided into numerous strips, some of them no wider than five yards. The manor was held either by an individual of means and standing, from the king down to a simple knight and a prosperous burgher, or by an institution such as a monastery, church, or college. Since the holder did not personally engage in the ignoble task of cultivating the land, he had other people do the work for him. These were the peasants, humble folk in various conditions of dependence on him, from the free to the unfree. But instead of hiring them to cultivate the entire arable for his own profit, he parceled out a large portion of it among them, not to own or to rent, but to farm for their own gain. In return for the use of these parcels, the peasants assumed certain obligations toward the manor lord. The exact amounts of these obligations varied from place to place, for they depended on the status of the peasant, on the custom of the manor, and on the size of the peasant's holding. But in general the peasants gave some portion of the produce they raised, made token payments in cash and in kind which signalized their bondage to the manor and their dependence on the lord, and worked a certain number of days per week or per season on the lord's demesne and on the manor buildings. In this way both the manor lord and the peasants raised their basic needs, the lord for his household and for the manorial establishment, and the peasants for their families. Surpluses, if any, were either stocked or taken to the local market to be sold for money or to be bartered for commodities which could not be raised on the manor. This whole system of relations and operations was held fast by custom which passed from generation to generation and so perpetuated it.

During the Renaissance period this system continued in several large sections of western and central Europe. It was prevalent in Catalonia;

in eastern and central France; in parts of Westphalia, Bavaria, and Austria, especially on monastic lands; and in Sweden. It was even present in more commercialized areas, in some sections of Genoese territory, for example, where, as late as the middle of the fifteenth century, peasants were still called serfs, were bound to the manors, passed their status to their offspring, paid the capitation tax as a sign of their bondage, paid the *taille,* and were subject to their lord's rights of justice and his banalities.[6]

Present and persisting in some regions in the west, manorialism and serfdom were actually gaining ground in eastern Europe, in Germany east of the Elbe, in Hungary, and in Poland. The extensive colonization in these areas in the later Middle Ages had opened up much new land. Then came the plagues, the Hussite wars, and the conflict between Poland and the Teutonic Knights, decimating the population and creating a shortage of labor. To hold on to at least some of their tenants, the landlords started restricting the latter's freedom of movement and imposing forced labor on them. Subsequently, in the late fifteenth and early sixteenth centuries, they intensified these restrictions: to take advantage of the upturn in the grain market due to the recovery of the population, they began to expand demesnial farming and, to assure themselves of the necessary labor without having to meet the rise in wages brought about by the accompanying inflationary trend, they quite naturally resorted to the policy of reducing their tenants to bondmen. And there was no one to say them nay since the authority of the central governments in these lands was declining in relation to their own. Hence with no one to turn to for protection, the peasantry had to accept subjection, and serfdom became the order of the day.[7]

CHANGES IN THE MANORIAL SYSTEM Elsewhere in western Europe manorialism was undergoing considerable transformation. A combination of influences, such as the growing desire of the manor lords to get more revenue from their manors, the simultaneous aspiration of the peasants for freedom from as many restrictions as possible, the shortage of labor due to repeated visitations of the plague, and various other economic and political exigencies began to impose strains on the system and forced several significant changes in it.[8]

One change which occurred was the gradual conversion of the servile labor services into money payments. To raise cash or to preclude the flight of the peasants to places where obligations were lighter or to towns where after a year and a day they could acquire freedom, the lord allowed his peasants to commute their *corvées* for payments in cash. Significant in itself, this change had a consequence which was even more important, namely, the elimination of bondage. So long as the peasants met their commutation payments, the lord had no reason to insist on their attachment to the manor. Commutation, therefore, led directly to the transformation of bondmen into freemen.

Another change was the gradual disappearance of the demesne. In the early days of the manorial system, when the acquisition of produce seemed essential, the lords generally reserved parts of the manor to be operated for their own benefit. Now, however, they found the demesne less valuable. Those who were allowing the commutation of *corvées* had to hire substitute workers to operate the demesne, and labor cost money; while the others who were reluctant to adopt commutation soon discovered that the demesne was a constant source of friction between them and the peasants who had to work it. Experience therefore dictated the advisability of reducing or even of discontinuing the demesne, and the lords soon adopted two methods of dispensing with it. They either leased it in its entirety to some enterprising renter in return for half the crop or for cash, or rented it in small parcels to a number of their own peasants. The result was the reduction or even the disappearance of *corvées* and of serfdom and the multiplication of the tenant class.

Both these changes led to a third change, namely, the transformation of the manor lord from a farm operator, with all that personal management entailed, into a lessor whose main interest was the collection of rents, whether in kind or in cash. But as a rent collector who was giving up the demesne and the *corvées* and who, incidentally, was also becoming an absentee landlord, the lord had less reason to insist on his rights of jurisdiction, and so these rights began to atrophy. This resulted in further disintegration of the manor.

If in some places the lord was detaching himself, so to speak, from the manor, there were other places where the lord was trying to become the sole exploiter of the entire manor or a part thereof. The motive naturally was profit. Where sheep raising was replacing grain growing or where the demands of the local market called for production of some special crop, the lord saw opportunities for gain and began to gather as much of the manor into his hands as possible. He exchanged some of his strips in one part of the field for others contiguous to his holdings in another part of the field; he pre-empted for his own use the villagers' right of pasture on the commons; and he appropriated the holdings of his serfs either through purchase or dispossession or occupation by right of reversion. The lands so accumulated he enclosed for a sheep-run or for growing a specialized crop and operated either with hired labor for his own profit. Sometimes the serfs followed his example. The result was that the manor either became a unified estate without any serfs on it or was broken up into a number of individually operated units with serfs as owners or tenants. In either case the old manor disappeared.

One additional development should be mentioned here, which, though not in the nature of a change, was nevertheless a factor in this transformation. This was the notable increase in the acquisition of lands by the bourgeois class, particularly by merchants and administrative officials who had some capital and an eye for profit and often also a hankering for a place in polite society, and who saw in land an answer to their pockets and their aspirations. Accordingly, they took advantage of the availability of farmlands on the market as a result of the progressive dissolution of the manorial system described above and acquired some by purchase or lease as their interests dictated. And if they did not buy the land or lease it, they gained possession of it by first advancing loans to the landlords on the security of their lands and then holding on to the same when the loans were not repaid; just so, for example, Jehan Guillaut, notary of Poitiers, acquired seven pieces of land from Joachim Gillier, knight and seigneur of Paygarreaux in Poitou, when the latter failed to repay the two loans which he had secured from Guillaut, one of 2,000 *livres* in 1522, and another of 800 *livres* six years later. And when they acquired these lands, they sought to make them profitable by putting them under businesslike management, which generally required the implementation of the changes outlined above.

Thus not only was a new class of landowners making its appearance, but the very entry of this new type of profit-minded proprietors further stimulated the very changes which got the class into landholding in the first place.

While all these developments were occurring during the Renaissance, it would be incorrect to identfy them narrowly with the Renaissance period, or to assume that they had a revolutionary effect on Renaissance economy.

In the first place, it should be recalled that there were sizable areas of Europe where these changes were absent during the Renaissance and other regions where manorialism was just beginning.

In the second place, in areas where these changes were transpiring, they were continuations or accentuations of trends which began some two centuries before the Renaissance. Ever since the rise of towns, from the eleventh century on, the manor lords, pressed for money, turned to their major source of income, their manors, and adopted a number of practices which started this whole movement of enfranchisement. They commuted labor services for cash; they opened virgin lands to colonization, and to attract settlers they offered the holdings not on the basis of the traditional *corvées* but in return for a share of the crop or for cash; they leased parts of their demesne on the same basis; and they sold "liberties" to their serfs, ostensibly for the good of their souls but really for the good of their purses. Sometimes they even pressed these "liberties" upon their serfs. It has been discovered, for example, that in France, in the reigns of Louis VI and Louis VII, the serfs had difficulty in obtaining their freedom, that under Philip the Fair it was offered to them, and that Louis X actually attempted to force it on them.[9] Hence enfranchisement of serfs and the origins of the accompanying manorial dissolution began before the Renaissance. The Renaissance merely saw the continuation of this trend.

In the third place, these changes, wherever they took place, though significant socially and legally, did not have profound transforming effects on the agricultural economy. For this there were two important reasons. First, only a small percentage of the arable and the pasture was enclosed during the Renaissance. While the enclosure movement provoked widespread and vehement denunciation as a revolutionary move-

ment destructive of peasant farming — and, indeed, it brought suffering
to those who lost their holdings — the extent of these enclosures was not
as great as the clamor against them might imply. In England, where
this movement went further than elsewhere, not more than 6 per cent
of the land was enclosed during the Renaissance period.[10] Second, the
conversion of serfs into tenant farmers did not immediately alter the
manner of farming nor increase substantially the income from the
manors. In England, again for example, where the greatest change
might be expected because the transformation of the peasant status was
more advanced than in the rest of Europe, there was no general abandonment of farming in common for farming "in several."[11] Moreover,
even where the latter method was adopted it did not necessarily result in
increased production, as often the holdings of the new tenants were no
larger than the farms they formerly held as serfs while, at the same
time, their resources individually were less adequate for the full exploitation of their lands than the resources of the manor collectively.[12]
True that many of the peasants were able to expand their few acres into
substantial holdings and thereby to produce sizable surpluses for the
market, but relatively the number of such successful tenants was still
small during the Renaissance. The great majority of the new tenants
merely held on to their scanty ancestral acres and continued largely as
subsistence farmers. They may have obtained their freedom, but with
their limited holdings and capital they were in no position to revolutionize agriculture in the Renaissance.

Perhaps one of the clearest indications that tenant farming did not
necessarily produce a prosperous tenantry was the state of the peasantry
in Renaissance Italy. As suggested earlier, north and central Italy had
relatively little manorialism, certainly from the thirteenth century on.
Farms were leased out to free tenants either on long-term leases which
were alienable or on short-term leases known as *mezzadria*. The latter,
which were a form of sharecropping with the proprietor providing some
stock and seed and the tenant doing all the work,[13] gradually displaced
the long-term leases and became the prevailing form during the Renaissance. However, irrespective of the type of lease under which the peasant operated the farm, he seems to have been unable to find prosperity.
There was small prospect, for example, in a lease of 1386 which re-

quired the tenant to "keep one ox and one ass" for use on the property
— which incidentally he could only buy with money advanced by the
owner of the farm — and raise one pig at half cost to himself and half
to the owner and then share it with him when it was grown and fat.
Indeed, the lease proved unacceptable to one tenant, for the record ends
with the statement "they went away and we granted the said farm to
Sandro." Sandro, it appears, held it for six years, and tried again in
1414 but "gave it up at the end of the year." Whether Sandro found a
more profitable lease elsewhere, which was not likely as this was more
or less typical, or ended a total failure is not known. But the latter consequence was not unlikely, if the following statement by a member of
the family who owned the land referred to in the above lease is any
indication:

> Piero and Mona Cilia are still alive and both infirm. I have let the
> farm for the coming year and I must set it in order; if those two old
> people were not to die, they will have to go and beg.[14]

So the price of a lifetime of tenant-farming in Italy could turn out
to be "beggary."

A less woeful picture, but one which supports our argument, comes
from England. On the lands of the Pastons, in the second half of the
fifteenth century, tenants frequently had their possessions destrained
for failure to meet their rent or were driven out. The following report
which was submitted to the Pastons by their steward is a most revealing
illustration:

> As to Skilly, farmer of Cowhow, we entered there and said we would
> have payment for the half-year past and surety for the half-year com-
> ing, or else we would destrain and put him out of possession and put
> in a new farmer.[15]

Skilly apparently stayed off the threat for the time being by promising
to pay a portion of the rent within two weeks. But even if he was not
driven off, the threat of eviction hung over his head, as over the heads
of many others in his circumstances, and that surely was a direful prospect.

Another example may be taken from a later date, about a century
and a half later. In 1634, in a court action concerning the customs of
the manor of Dent, Yorkshire, an octogenarian reported that tenements

which were not devised by the owner's will descended "to all his sons equally to be divided amongst them," wherefore, he added, "the tenants are much increased in number more than they were, and the tenements become so small in quantity that many of them are not above three or four acres a piece and generally not above eight or nine *so that they could not maintain their families* [italics added] were it not by their industry in knitting coarse stockings."[16]

The point then is clear. Unless one accumulated acre upon acre and farmed for his own profit, he was not likely to become prosperous. Tenant-farming on small farms did not hold much promise of material advancement even though the tenant was free.

SUMMARY Looking back at this survey of agriculture during the Renaissance, one can see some developments but no revolution. Neither in techniques of farming, nor in the acreage involved, nor in the science of farming, nor in the yield was there any significant change. There was considerable change in the organizational system of farming: the manor was broken up among individual tenants, or it was being enclosed as a single unit. However, the change was more pronounced in its social effects than in its economic effects. For while bondmen farmers were being converted into free tenant farmers, the former subsistence farming on small plots with inadequate stock and equipment remained practically unchanged; only a small percentage of the new tenants became prosperous enough to operate "commercialized" farms. Furthermore, both the conversion of serfs into free peasants and farming for the sake of profit were not Renaissance innovations but continuations from the Middle Ages.[17]

Stock Raising and Sheep Ranching

STOCK RAISING After farming and market gardening, stock raising was next in importance. Most of the peasants combined farming with the raising of some stock. A milk cow or two, a goat, a team of oxen, perhaps a horse, several sheep, and one or two hogs were to be found on the farms of many of the peasants.[18] The manor had more of the same. This stock supplied draught power for farm needs, hides for leather goods, fleece for clothing, and food products, and made life for their owners more tolerable.

Prevalent as was this supplementary raising of stock, it could hardly be considered a form of industry, as it was conducted haphazardly. Its operation was both age-old and natural, and needs no elaboration. More important was the large-scale sheep ranching, and this deserves fuller consideration.

SHEEP RANCHING The growth of population during the Middle Ages and its concentration in towns, combined with the steady improvement of political order and of transportation on land and sea, increased the demand for wool; hence sheep raising became an important industry. While all European lands engaged in this industry, especially in those regions where grain farming was impractical, some countries soon outstripped others.

England was one of these. Its extensive downs provided ample pasturage. Its damp climate made the fleece less breakable in the spinning operations. Its proximity to urbanized Flanders, the center of cloth industry in northern Europe in medieval times, provided it with a ready market. Its contact with Italy through the papal tax-collectors, who often were associates of Italian merchant-bankers engaged in wool and cloth trade, opened an additional market. Finally, from the early fourteenth century on, when England decided to increase the manufacture of its own cloth, it was able to dispose of the finished products on the markets of eastern Europe. This steady demand for English wool and cloth naturally promoted the industry and in the end led to some withdrawal of land from grain growing in favor of sheep raising.

Spain was another country where this industry became important. Two factors contributed to its development there. One was the abundance of unsettled or sparsely settled land, due either to the unsuitability of the terrain for agriculture or to the devastations caused by the raids and counter-raids as part of the *Reconquista.* The other was the introduction of the merino breed of sheep by the African tribe Benimerines in the course of the Almohad invasion about the middle of the twelfth century. It was an excellent wool-producing breed, both as to quantity and quality of the wool. The merits of its fleece were soon discovered by Europe's cloth manufacturers, and the resulting continent-wide demand for it naturally led to the expansion of sheep raising in Spain.

Then when the Castilian kings discovered in this industry a sure and steady source of tax income, they gave it further encouragement by enacting favorable legislation, particularly as to provisions for pasturage.

Southern France, especially in the regions bordering on the Pyrennes and the Alps, and southern Italy with the extensive dry lands in Apulia were two other regions where sheep ranching attained the proportions of a real industry.

In all the lands which engaged in large-scale sheep ranching, in addition to the small flocks owned by the peasant farmers, there were medium-sized flocks owned by more prosperous proprietors, some of whom were bourgeois speculators, and large flocks, numbering in the hundreds and even thousands of sheep, owned by nobles or by religious institutions, mostly monasteries. For the latter two groups this enterprise was big business, organized in a businesslike way. Summer and winter pasturage was procured if transhumation was practiced; if not, the fold was moved from the grazed to the ungrazed sections of the estate; shepherds were engaged to tend the flocks, geld the lambs, and brand the animals with the owner's mark; shelters, washing pens, and storage facilities were erected; shearers were hired to shear the animals; and the fleeces were wound and prepared for the market.[19]

Perhaps the best organized sheep-ranching industry was that in Spain. There, because of the long distances between summer and winter pasturages — in the northern part of the peninsula in summer and the southern in the winter — and the difficulties entailed by this long trek across the peninsula, the sheep raisers organized themselves in a gild known as the Mesta.[20] It included small ranchers who herded their own flocks, and larger ranchers with thousands of sheep who hired shepherds with assistants and sheep dogs to tend their flocks. The gild drew up strict by-laws governing the industry and enforced them rigorously, and it was influential enough to secure royal recognition and regular confirmations of its charter.

The trek southward began about the middle of September. It was carefully supervised by shepherds and overseers and moved along legally prescribed trails, halting from time to time for the flocks to graze on the open countryside along the trails. The trek took about two months. In the south, the sheep were pastured on unsettled royal lands, unclaimed territory, and on rented, private grazing grounds. The return trek started about the middle of April. Along the way, stops were made at gild sheds to have the sheep sheared. Clippers worked in large groups, sometimes including as many as 125 men capable of shearing up to 1,000 sheep a day. The wool was either sold as clipped, or washed and stored in warehouses to be marketed later when the market was not glutted. The return was completed by early June, when the season terminated. This was repeated annually.

Once the merino breed was adopted, the owners worked diligently at improving their stock. They culled the scrub animals and the barren ewes and bred scientifically until they acquired a satisfactory flock.

This method of ranching and the organization of the Mesta were of long standing. Their early beginnings are traceable back to the time of the Visigoths, but their rapid development came in the Middle Ages as the frontiers of the Moors were pushed back. It was a completed system by the fourteenth century. Except for some expansion in size, it continued without any great changes throughout the Renaissance period.

Abbreviations used in this and in the subsequent chapters are:

AHR — *The American Historical Review*
CEcH — *The Cambridge Economic History of Europe*
EcHR — *The Economic History Review*
RB   — *Revue belge de philologie et d'histoire*

1. On these revolutions see Lynn White, Jr., *Medieval Technology and Social Change* (Oxford: Clarendon Press, 1962), first two chapters.

2. This is the thesis of Roger Dion, *Histoire de la vigne et du vin en France, des origines au xixe siècle* (Paris, 1959). Cf. G. Duby's review of the work in *EcHR*, XIII (1960), 162–3. Very valuable on this subject is M. Mollat *et al.*, "L'économie Européenne aux deux derniers siècles du moyen-âge," *Storia del medioevo*, vol. III of *Relazioni del X congresso internazionale di scienze storiche* (Firenze: G. C. Sansoni-Editore, no date), 685–92.

3. Marcel Delafosse, "Les vignerons d'auxerrois, xive–xvie siècles," *Annales de Bourgogne*, XX (1948), 59; Jacques Boussard, "La vie en Anjou aux xie et xiie siècles," *Le moyen âge*, LVI (1950), 59; Eleanor Lodge, "The Estates of the Archbishop and Chapter of Saint-André of Bordeaux under English Rule," vol. III of *Oxford Studies in Social and Legal History* (1912), 160; Robert Boutruche, *La crise d'une so-*

ciété. Seigneurs et paysans du Bordelais pendant la Guerre de Cents Ans (Paris: Société d'éditions les belles lettres, 1957), 32–35.

4. On the abandonment of farmlands see Georges Duby, *L'économie rurale et la vie des campagnes dans l'occident médiéval* (Paris: Éditions Montaigne, 1962), II, 556–8. On the lack of clearing of new lands see *The Cambridge Medieval History*, VII, 724–7; Marc Bloch, *Les caractères originaux de l'histoire rurale française* (Oslo: H. Aschehoug & Co., 1931), 5–19; Prosper Boissonnade, *Life and Work in Medieval Europe*, trans. Eileen Power (New York: Alfred A. Knopf, 1927), 226–31. On land drainage and reclamation in the sixteenth century see Charles Singer *et al.* (eds.), *A History of Technology* (Oxford: Clarendon Press, 1957), III, 300–23.

5. Cf. P. J. Jones, "An Italian Estate, 900–1200," *EcHR*, 2d series, VII (1954), 18–32.

6. See Jacques Heers, *Gênes au xvᵉ siècle, École pratique des hautes études* — VIᵉ section. *Centre de recherches historiques, Affaires et gens d'affaires*, XXIV (Paris: S. E. V. P. E. N., 1961), 524–31.

7. On the existence of serfdom in Europe during the Renaissance see *The Cambridge Medieval History*, VII, 731–9; Jacob Salwyn Shapiro, *Social Reform and the Reformation*, vol. XC of *Studies in History, Economics and Public Law* (New York: Columbia University Press, 1900), 45–62; Francis L. Carsten, *The Origins of Prussia* (Oxford: Clarendon Press, 1954), chap. viii, "The Agrarian Crisis," and chap. xi, "Decline of the Peasantry and the Imposition of Serfdom." Especially valuable is Jerome Blum's "The Rise of Serfdom in Eastern Europe," *AHR*, LXII (1957), 807–36.

8. For a fuller treatment of these changes see Duby, *op. cit.*, II, 581–611; *CEcH*, vol. I, *The Agrarian Life of the Middle Ages* (Cambridge: Cambridge University Press, 1941), 317–22, 493–561; Marc Bloch, *op. cit.*, 95–154, and his more recent *Seigneurie française et manoir anglais* (Paris: Librairie Armand Colin, 1960); R. H. Tawney, *The Agrarian Problem in the Sixteenth Century* (London: Longmans, Green and Co., 1912). Cf. also Yvonne Bezard, *La vie rurale dans le sud de la region parisienne de 1450 à 1560* (Paris: Librairie de Paris, Firmin-Didot et cie., 1929), 68–71, 75–78; Paul Raveau, *L'agriculture et les classes paysannes. La transformation de la propriété dans le haut Poitou au xviᵉ siècle* (Paris: Librairie des sciences politiques et sociales, 1926), 116–26, 292–5; Charles Stewart Orwin, *A History of English Farming* (London: Thomas Nelson & Sons, Ltd., 1949), 25–35; and M. M. Postan's review of L. Genicot's *L'économie rurale Namuroise au bas moyen âge — 1199–1429* (Namur, 1943) in *EcHR*, 2d series, II (1950), 326–7.

9. Marc Bloch, *Rois et serfs* (Paris: Librairie ancienne Honore Champion, 1920). 174.

10. E. Lipson, *The Economic History of England,* vol. I, *The Middle Ages* (6th ed.; London: A. C. Black, Ltd., 1935), 158–60. Cf. also L. A. Parker, "The Agrarian Revolution at Cotesbach, 1501–1612," *Studies in Leicestershire Agrarian History,* ed. W. G. Hoskins (Leicestershire Archaeological Society, 1949), who shows that in this region the real revolution came after the Tudor period.

11. Muriel St. Clare Byrne, *Elizabethan Life in Town and Country* (3d ed.; London: Methuen & Co., Ltd., 1941), 106–8.

12. See M. M. Postan, "The Fifteenth Century," *EcHR,* IX (1939), 162–3.

13. The contract is reproduced in full in Marchesa Niccolini's article, "A Medieval Florentine, his Family and his Possessions," *AHR,* XXXI (1925), 1–20. The contract appears on 14–16.

14. *Ibid.,* 17–18.

15. *The Paston Letters, 1422–1509,* ed. James Gairdner (London, 1901), no. 284. For an illuminating depiction of peasant life in Paston's England see H. S. Bennett, *The Pastons and Their England* (2d ed.; Cambridge: University Press, 1932), 250–60.

16. Cited from Joan Thirsk, "Industries in the Countryside," *Essays in the Economic and Social History of Tudor and Stuart England in Honor of R. H. Tawney,* ed. F. J. Fisher (Cambridge: University Press, 1961), 70.

17. While no one account of a manor can be singled out as the most illustrative of the actual developments in manorialism during the Renaissance, perhaps the clearest exposition available, one which reveals the changes and at the same time the slowness of these changes, is Arthur Gough Ruston's and Denis Witney's *Hooton Pagnell. The Agricultural Evolution of a Yorkshire Village* (New York: Longmans, Green & Co., 1934).

18. Cf. M. M. Postan, "Village Livestock in the Thirteenth Century," *EcHR,* 2d series, XV (1962), 219–49. Although too early for our period, the article is highly suggestive.

19. For an account of these operations in England in the Tudor period see Peter J. Bowden, *The Wool Trade in Tudor and Stuart England* (London: Macmillan & Co., Ltd., 1962), 1–40. Cf. also K. J. Allison, "Flock Management in the Sixteenth and Seventeenth Centuries," *EcHR,* 2d series, XI (1958), 98–112.

20. On the history of the Mesta and its operations see Julius Klein, *The Mesta. A Study in Spanish Economic History 1273–1836,* vol. XXI of *Harvard Economic Studies* (Cambridge: Harvard University Press, 1920).

CHAPTER II *Commerce and Related Business Institutions and Instruments*

Local and Extra-Local Commerce

NEXT TO agriculture and stock raising the most important economic enterprise of the people during the centuries of the Renaissance was commerce, the buying and selling of goods. To appreciate its nature and scope it is necessary to examine not only the growth of commerce and the innovations in connection with its pursuit, but also its normal operations.

LOCAL COMMERCE If we cast our eyes on the customary, day-to-day, commercial operations of the Renaissance period, we shall quickly discover that the bulk of commerce was still local in scope. Peasants brought their produce of the field, garden, and pasture to the local market and sold it to the local townsmen. In return, they procured their needs from the local craftsmen: heavy cloaks from the local tailor, headwear from the local hatters, footwear from the local shoemakers, metal implements of the field and garden from the local smiths, earthenware from the local potters, knives from the local cutler, and so on. Townsmen for the most part met their wants in the same way. They sold their wares and services on the home market and procured their needs from local craftsmen and merchants operating in the same market. There were of course business transactions between tradesmen and entrepreneurs who supplied commodities of nonlocal provenience or who exported the tradesmen's products abroad, but this inter-regional commerce certainly did not displace or surpass commerce which was strictly local in character. Now if we recall that the peasantry and the urban proletariat together constituted the great majority of the population, we cannot escape the conclusion that local commerce was still the prevailing type of commerce during the Renaissance epoch.

NATIONAL AND INTERNATIONAL COMMERCE But while much of the commerce in the Renaissance period was still local in scope, a considerable percentage of it, and a growing percentage, was national and international in range. Some staples, even such universal ones as grain, could not be raised in sufficient quantities everywhere and had to be imported from wherever possible, sometimes from distant areas. Thus, Genoa and the towns in its territory were flanked by rocky terrain not suitable for agriculture, and so their 100,000 inhabitants had to depend on imported wheat, mainly from Provence, Sicily and the Maghreb, some from Ukraine, and some, their respective governments permitting, from Tuscany and Naples.[1] Then there were certain commodities which were produced in only a few places but were used universally and so had to be distributed over wide areas. Salt, for instance, indispensable as an appetizer and as a preservative of meats, was not obtainable everywhere; it was processed on the salt flats of the northern Adriatic, southern Castile, Bay of Biscay, and on the northeast coast of England; or it was mined in such places as Halle in Tyrol, Wieliczka in Poland, and Salins in Franche-Comté. From these several localities it had to be distributed throughout the entire continent, and so commerce in salt became European-wide. Fish may be taken as another commodity that was subject to similar conditions. Herring was caught in the waters of the North Sea and in the straits separating the Scandinavian peninsula from the mainland, and cod came from the Banks of Newfoundland. Since all Europe needed fish — for the lenten days were numerous, and meats would not keep as long as dried, salted fish — it necessarily became a commodity of national and international commerce. Cotton, spices and incense, except for some small quantities of the latter, were not produced in Europe but came from the Near East, from Abyssinia and India and the distant Indies; and so they, too, entered the stream of international commerce. Next to goods whose restricted provenience made for international commerce were goods whose superiority to similar domestic products won for them both national and international markets. Thus, while much of the continent tried to produce its own wines, the more palatable wines from Aquitaine, Poitou, and Burgundy (particularly in the region of Beauné) soon appeared to command many of the markets in western Europe.[2] Similarly, because the wools of

England and Spain were found to be superior to wools raised elsewhere in Europe, they were much in demand from the North Sea to Italy. Likewise the red cloth of Florence, the silks of Genoa and Florence, the linen of Hainaut, the glass of Venice, the fustians of south Germany, the woad of Provence, the leather goods of Cordova, the furs and hemp of the Baltic lands, the rich cloth and the rugs and lacquered goods of the Near and the Far East — all were deemed more desirable than the corresponding domestic products, and so they entered into the streams of national and international commerce. Finally, there was, of course, the reverse flow of goods and bullion necessary to meet the cost of the various wares and commodities mentioned above. Thus, for example, in 1377 Genoa exported to Alexandria gold thread valued at 2,925 *lire*; in 1459 a merchant of Barcelona transported 4,000 ducats of gold to the same city; and in 1495–1496 the Venetian galleys sailed for Alexandria with 500 casks of wine, 1,100,000 pounds of copper, and 190,000 ducats in cash.

An excellent illustration of one stream of this international trade is that which Florence had with England and Flanders in the fifteenth century.[3]

From Pisa, the port of Florence, the state galleys carrying some luxury goods — satins, silks, brocades, thread of gold, gold and silver utensils — and sometimes alum (from 1463), spices, and wine stopped at a number of ports in southern France and Spain to pick up additional cargo of rice, almonds, woad, saffron, olive oil, soap, and raw silk and proceeded via Dartmouth, where they revictualed, to Flanders (Sluys) where they disposed of part of their luxury items and picked up some goods — general merchandise, tapestry, head gear, and Baltic furs and feathers — in exchange. In the fifteenth century this was only a small portion, perhaps less than a tenth of the total value of the Florentine cargo. From Sluys the ships proceeded to Southampton, discharged the rest of their cargo, loaded up with cloth, lead, tin, but mostly with wool, and sailed for home by way of Barcelona.

When the value of the cargo which the Florentines sold in England approximated the value of the goods they purchased there, the problem of payment did not arise. But when there was an imbalance in favor of the English sellers, as happened often, then payments had to be made in bills drawn on Florentine banking houses in Bruges where the English were heavy customers. And when the imbalance in the Flemish trade was in favor of the Florentines, then the Flemish buyers paid in bills drawn on their agents in Barcelona with whom they had a favorable balance of trade but with whom the Florentines on the contrary had an unfavorable balance. In this way the circuit was completed.

Although only a single example, this stream is quite illustrative of the character of international trade during the Renaissance period. All that needs to be added for a more comprehensive picture of this trade is the reminder that there were other streams paralleling this Florentine traffic and linking with each other. Thus there were Venetian, Genoese, and Argonese streams connecting the Mediterranean seaports with Europe, and similar currents which joined the Baltic towns with Flanders, England, France, and Spain. Then there were a number of riverine streams which paralleled or webbed this maritime traffic and several overland streams using pack animals or wagons which linked northern Europe with Italy by way of the Alpine passes. Finally there were a number of inland towns, Lyon and Geneva especially, which served as "clearing house" centers for the cross-country trade in the same way as Barcelona served for the Florentine trade with the west and north.[4]

MEDIEVAL ORIGINS OF EXTRA-LOCAL COMMERCE This extra-local trade was, of course, not an innovation of the Renaissance. Never absent totally, not even in the darkest days of the early Middle Ages, it had been increasing steadily from the tenth century, and by the beginning of the Renaissance it had reached substantial proportions.[5] The traders of Venice, Genoa, Pisa, Marseilles, and Catalonia were tapping the trade of the Near East and North Africa and distributing it to all points in western Europe. Those of Bordeaux, Nantes, Rouen, and of the English ports ranged from Lisbon to Flanders; and those of the German Hansa extended the link deep into the Baltic. Iberian ports, both on the Mediterranean and on the Atlantic, were attracting merchants from Italy, Flanders, France, Germany, and England and made of Portugal "a wharf between two seas."[6] In the heart of western Europe, the famous fairs of Champagne long served as recognized international markets where men from all corners of the continent assembled to transact business. Wines of Aquitaine were found on the tables from Spain to Scandinavia as early as the 1200's, and in the early decades of the fourteenth century the volume exported reached the astounding total of 90,000 to 100,000 tons. In the same way English wool, always present on the continent throughout the Middle Ages, actually reached its maximum export volume of approximately 32,000 sacks as early as 1273.[7] Similarly the cloth of Arras, Ypres, and Ghent, the copper and brass wares of Dinant, the woad of Picardy and Toulouse, and the alum of Crete[8] were to be found on the markets of western Europe from the twelfth and thirteenth centuries. Thus, national and international commerce was well established before the advent of the Renaissance.

If the Renaissance period inherited national and international commerce from the Middle Ages, it does not follow that the inheritance remained unchanged. On the other hand, the label "Renaissance," presupposing rebirth or revival, should not lead us to expect revolutionary changes.

Changes from Medieval Commerce

COMMERCE WITH NEWLY DISCOVERED LANDS One change, an obvious one, was the opening of new markets in Africa, in the Orient, and in the New World. Starting in the early fifteenth century, Portuguese sailors moved southward along the coast of Africa, rounded the Cape of Good Hope in 1498, reached India and the East Indies in the next two decades and Japan by 1550. All along they established trade contacts. From the coasts of equatorial Africa they got gold dust, ivory, and slaves; from India, oriental luxuries; and from the Indies, spices — pepper in particular. About the same time, the Spaniards, following the example of Portugal, explored Central America, Mexico, and South America and traded manufactured supplies, cattle, grain, flour, wine, and slaves for the New World's silver, gold, tropical medicinal herbs, and other commodities. The French and the English contributed little or nothing at all to the opening of North America during the Renaissance despite the voyages of the Cabots for England and of Cartier for France. However, as part of this overseas commercial expansion the English under Chancellor struck north of Scandinavia and opened up direct commerce with Russia via the White Sea, thereby by-passing the Hansa middlemen.

Dramatic as this opening of the new markets may appear, its impact on Renaissance commerce and economy was not substantial, certainly not before the middle of the sixteenth century. In the first place, the risks involved and the time consumed in these distant overseas ventures were great and often precluded possibilities of profit. In 1530, for example, the Portuguese estimated that they lost 300 ships. If some adventurers were fortunate to escape the dangers and so made great profits, the "killings" that they made were insufficient to effect a transformation of national economies. Secondly, most of the opening occurred in the sixteenth century, that is at the end of the Renaissance, and in its initial stages it did not produce sufficient volume of trade to cause a significant impact. Spain, for example, as late as 1550, was dispatching only between 50 and 60 small ships of about 100 tons average annually to the New World,[9] and this did not generate enough tonnage to affect substantially the commerce of a nation the size of Spain. What impact there was resulted from the increasing amount of precious metals that this shipping brought from Mexico and Peru. But this influx had adverse effects, for it fanned inflation which spread from Spain to the rest of Europe and caused considerable economic dislocation everywhere. Moreover, even this impact did not reach significant proportions until the second half of the sixteenth century. During the Renaissance period proper, Portugal alone seems to have felt the commercial consequences of the newly opened overseas trade, its near-monopoly of the spice trade bringing great wealth to its capital. And to the extent that Antwerp was made the distributing center for this spice trade, it, too, profited from this new overeas trade.

A by-product of this opening of the new markets was the eclipse of the Italian cities as the principal entrepots of European commerce. Throughout the Middle Ages and the first century of the Renaissance they throve in part as commercial intermediaries between western Europe and the Levant. But with the curtailment of the Levantine trade because of the Turkish conquests of the Italian outposts in the eastern Mediterranean and with the discovery by the westerners of new markets along the west coast of Africa, in the east around Africa, and in the Americas, the Italian cities naturally lost their role as middlemen and so began to decline. On the other hand, western European ports began to rise in commercial prominence. Cadiz, Seville, Lisbon, Rochelle, Brest, Rouen, Bristol, London, and Antwerp were becoming the new commercial stars. And to the extent that this was actually happening during the Renaissance, it may be said that the Renaissance laid the basis for the economic map of modern Europe.

Specific illustrations of this shift from the Mediterranean to the north may be found in the decline of the fortunes of Venice, Florence, and Genoa in the commerce of northern Europe after 1450.

Venice, as we know, had been pumping economic lifeblood into Germany and central Europe from the tenth century on, and it was still doing so in the 1400's. By that time, however, it had helped to beget a number of enterprising German merchant-families — among them the Fuggers — who soon displaced it as the principal economic power in that part of Europe. And most of these traders, be it noted, gained this ascendancy not because they continued to trade with Venice but because they also turned to the city which was becoming the terminus and the hub of the oceanic trade, namely, Antwerp. Thus what Venice was to the German businessmen in the fifteenth century, Antwerp became in the sixteenth century, and much to the loss of Venice.

Fifteenth-century Florence under the Medici was still an important commercial center on the continent. The Medici had branches in Bruges and London and business connections elsewhere in northern Europe. There were, of course, other Florentine business firms with similar interests in the north; and together the Medici and their countrymen helped Florence maintain its economic role on the continent. We also noticed that it was in the fifteenth century that Florence inaugurated the policy of sending its own merchant fleet to England and Flanders. Whether the policy was undertaken to bolster a faltering economy or to expand a thriving economy, the action reveals the city's drive for European business. But this forward position was not sustained for long. Before the century was over the Medici branches failed and were not replaced. At the same time the trade with Southampton was invaded by London merchants who soon succeeded in reversing the stream by prevailing on Henry VII to wrest a treaty from Florence permitting English ships to carry wool to Pisa. Even though the resulting penetration of the Mediterranean by the English was still very small at this time, it was symptomatic nevertheless of the shift of economic preponderance from the Mediterranean to the North Sea.

Genoa's decline came somewhat later, but it was more drastic. Throughout the three centuries from the first crusade to 1375 Genoa concentrated on the Levantine trade and engaged in a desperate rivalry with Venice for control of this trade. But after its defeat in the War of Chioggia (1376–1380) it turned to regions where Venetian competition was less vigorous — to northern Africa and the Iberian Peninsula. Accordingly Genoese merchants and bankers and sailors became very active in these areas and actually participated under the crowns of Portugal and Spain in the opening of the African, Atlantic and the New World trade. This participation naturally brought some economic advantages to Genoa itself, and its fortune as an important center was thereby prolonged. In the end, however, it too yielded ground to Cadiz and Lisbon. As these cities developed their economic potential, their citizens began displacing the Genoese entrepreneurs to the detriment of Genoa's business. In addition, both these cities secured monopolies of the oceanic trade which naturally curtailed Genoa's participation still more. And what it did not lose as a result of these first two developments, it lost when it became involved in the Franco-Spanish wars over Italy on the side of France which suffered repeated defeats.

Thus by the end of the Renaissance, the three principal Italian cities, Venice, Florence, and Genoa, which had dominated European commerce for many centuries, lost this domination to the cities on the Atlantic and on the English Channel.

THE PROBLEM OF VOLUME Closely related to these developments is the matter of the volume of trade in the Renaissance period as compared with its magnitude in the preceding age. In the past, it was generally assumed that the Renaissance age witnessed a steady and a substantial increase in commerce. This assumption is no longer held, for recent studies have shown that instead of a constant rise there actually were two opposite trends. During the first half of the Renaissance period, roughly from about 1325 until 1450, the trend was downward — a rather sharp decline. Thereafter the trend turned upward, rose substantially, and by the end of the Ranaissance period it was reaching and exceeding the pre-depression level. Of course, the pattern of decline and recovery was not a uniform one: some cities undoubtedly saw the recovery sooner, while others, later, or perhaps not at all. In Genoa, for example, the tide turned about half a century earlier, and the revival, although intermittent, was substantial. On the other hand, Bruges had practically no recovery during the last decades of the Renaissance period, since Antwerp replaced it as the principal entrepot in the north. But these variations to the contrary notwithstanding, the picture of decline and revival in western Europe as a whole certainly holds true.

The extent of the decline cannot be ascertained readily because statistical data for the first half of the Renaissance period are quite scarce. But where such evidence is available, as in the case of partial customs accounts of some cities, it generally reflects a substantial downward trend. For example, in Pera, a suburb of Constantinople which served as a Genoese entrepot for Byzantine trade, "taxes levied on maritime trade . . . fell from £1,648,630 Gen. in 1334 to £1,199,046 in 1391 and £234,000 in 1423," and in Genoa itself taxable commerce that moved through its port dropped from £3,822,000 Gen. in 1293 to £887,000 in 1424 and remained below the first figure throughout the Renaissance period. In Marseille wharfage dues fell by more than 100 per cent between the years 1358 and 1412, while cereal imports fell by more than 700 per cent between 1340 and 1412. Equally substantial drops are reported for Geneva, an inland entrepot for commerce between Italy and northern Europe, and for Bordeaux.[10] To these few examples chosen at random, others like them may be added, and still others which deal with activities related to commerce, such as industrial output and shipping;[11] and taken together, they all point to the conclusion that commercial activities declined substantially during the first century of the Renaissance period.[12]

For a decline of such proportions the causes had to be of considerable magnitude. There were several, and some of them operated simultaneously so that the combined impact was even greater.

One cause, and probably the greatest one, was the drop in population. Authorities on European demography tell us that the population of western Europe had been growing from the eleventh century until the first part of the fourteenth century; that this trend was reversed by the ravages of the Black Plague; that the recovery was slow; and that it was impeded by repeated visitations of the plague and by numerous protracted wars, particularly by the Hundred Years' War, the repeated wars between France and Burgundy for the Low Countries, the Swedish "liberation" wars, the wars between Poland and the Teutonic Knights, the various peasants' revolts, and the Turkish invasion into the heart of Europe. In Catalonia, for example, the number of homesteads dropped from 95,000 in 1365 to 59,000 in 1497 and was still 20,000 short in 1553.[13] In Barcelona, whereas there were 7,651 hearths in 1359 and 7,645 in 1378, there were only 6,432 hearths in 1515, and it was not until considerably after this date, probably not until the seventeenth century, that the figures of 1359 and 1378 were surpassed.[14] Palermo dropped from approximately 44,000 people in 1276 to about 25,000 in 1479; while Florence "fell from about 110,000 inhabitants in 1338 to 45–50,000 in 1351" and did not recover its original figure during the rest of the Renaissance, having some 70,000–75,000 in 1380 and the same number in 1526.[15] Toulouse dropped from about 30,000 in 1335 to some 20,000 in 1450; Marseille lost about three-fourths of its inhabitants; and in Provence many areas, hit by poverty and plagues, lost up to one-half of their population by 1351 and up to four-fifths by 1420.[16] Hainaut suffered a drop in its rural population from approximately 31,000 in 1365 to about 20,000 in 1440–1441, and did not regain the 30,000 figure until 1540–1541.[17] In England the figure reached approximately 3,700,000 in 1348, dropped to about 2,250,000 in 1377, and was still about a quarter of a million short of the 1348 figure in 1545.[18] The same is true of western Germany, where it has been shown that towns which had outgrown their medieval walls more than once during the eleventh, twelfth, and thirteenth centuries "usually stopped growing some time in the fourteenth from which time their area in most cases sufficed for their inhabitants until the nineteenth century."[19] Similar losses occurred in east Germany, Flanders, and Switzerland.[20] It is certain therefore that the population of western Europe during most of the Renaissance period was smaller than it was before the Black Plague, perhaps by as much as 25 per cent and possibly more. And since population numbers have a direct bearing on consumption, it is reasonable to assume that the volume of commerce, considered in the aggregate, must have declined correspondingly.

Another cause, perhaps second to the Plague in its adverse effects, was the widespread devastation caused by wars. As a result of the Hundred Years' War and its accompanying lawlessness, the devastation of France, that once-prosperous country, was truly catastrophic. Towns were sacked, villages were razed, cattle and movables were carried off, and large areas of arable were laid waste. In addition, production and employment declined and with them the nation's earning and purchasing power which in turn led to a further drop of production.[21] And so destitution and hopelessness set in where frugal prosperity and confidence once prevailed, and this condition lasted in some places even as late as 1484 when the Estates presented their picture of woe and want.[22] The wars in Italy, products of bitter interurban rivalry, were chronic and almost as ruinous. One has only to turn the pages of such town chronicles as that of Francesco Matarazzo of Perugia to see how terrible were the ravages. The Hussite wars in Bohemia, the German-Slav wars in eastern Germany, the numerous peasants' revolts, and the Turkish scourge in the Balkans brought similar ruin to much of central Europe. The prolonged conflict between Aragon and the Angevins, at first over Sicily and subsequently over Naples, disrupted trade in the western Mediterranean and eventually, in 1423, brought disaster to Marseille, which had become part of Provence, as the Aragonese sacked the city horribly. In Spain a bitter dynastic war dragged out interminably, roughly from 1350 to 1475, causing such distress that the period has been called the "Century of Troubles." England also suffered from a similar affliction, though somewhat later. From the 1450's until Henry VII's victory at Bosworth Field in 1485, the land was subjected to intermittent wars, the notorious Wars of the Roses, with adverse consequences for commerce. Although devastation itself was not extensive, the disruption of traffic and the uncertainties concerning commercial treaty rights held by alien merchants due to the fluctuating fortunes of the contending parties had depressing effects.[23] All these wars, harmful enough separately, were even more injurious collectively as several of them raged simultaneously and so extended and intensified the destruction. And coming on top of the Plague, their ruinous effects were truly dire.

Besides these two main reasons, there were of course lesser, contributory factors. One, about which there can be no question, was the impairment of trade with Asia in the early fourteenth century. In the previous century relations between the west and the various Mongol Khanates which extended from southern Russia and Persia to distant China were friendly, and this was reflected in the busy activities of western merchants, Genoese especially, at Tana, Caffa, Tabriz, Samarkand, and Trebizond whither Asiatic trade flowed in increasing quantity. The journeys of the Polo's all the way to remote Peking clearly signalize this east-west contact. But with the disruption of these Mongol states in the first four decades of the fourteenth century, topped by the collapse of the Khanate of China in 1368, the opportunities which the westerners enjoyed hitherto came to an end, and trade with Asia declined with noticeable repercussions in Mediterranean commerce.[24] Another factor, recently brought out, is that of a natural economic regression following a long period of rapid expansion. In the flush of the thirteenth-century growth, business and industry expanded beyond Europe's capacity to support them. In time, therefore, the point was reached when the pace slackened and regression set in. National bankruptcies of England and France, manipulation of coinage, bank failures (especially those of the Bardi and the Peruzzi), abandonment of lands of only marginal productivity, and a leveling off of population — all are evidenced in the early decades of the fourteenth century and all were signs of faltering economy.[25] While it is difficult to assess the extent of this regression, it is more than probable that coinciding with the decline in Asiatic trade it opened the way for the depression brought about by the main causes.

By the middle of the fifteenth century, the decline ceased and the curve turned upward and rose steadily with the usual normal dips. Customs and shipping records in western European countries reveal substantial increases despite occasional fluctuations.[26] Thus, shipping in northern Germany increased almost twofold between 1470 and 1570, rising from 60,000 to 110,000 tons, and that of the Low Countries almost quadrupled, from 60,000 to 232,000 tons.[27] By the end of the Renaissance period, then, the pre-depression level was reached and surpassed, except in Italy where the revival was interrupted by the wars unloosed by the French invasions and by the Turkish aggression in the eastern Mediterranean.

Perhaps the most important cause of the recovery was the resumption of the growth of population. This has been indicated already in the account depicting the decline. It was shown that once the critical stage of the plagues was turned the population decline was arrested and the trend reversed. By the end of the Renaissance period most countries had reached and some surpassed the pre-plague figures. Naturally this increase contributed to the recovery of commerce.

Not only was the population growing but the people were setting their living standards higher. The peasantry and the urban proletariat with little to sell to profit from the price rise in the sixteenth century did not improve their lot substantially,[28] but here and there some were beginning to add glass windows and chimneys to their houses, a silk ribbon or two to their dress, and a little sugar and more spices and meat to their diet. The middle class was indulging in excessive dress habits, even to the point of provoking repeated sumptuary laws which prohibited them from exceeding the standards proper to their class. The aristocracy, both noble and moneyed, often referred to as the "brilliant consumer" class, actually made it a habit, an art, and an objective to live extravagantly and sometimes even prodigally.[29] Their splendid residences, richly appointed, far surpassed the somber homes or castles of the Middle Ages. Their tables and cellars, as Sir Anthony Fitzherbert (1470–1538) relates, were stocked "fer above measure" with "delycyous meats, drinkes and spyces" at a cost "four tymes" as great as before; while their apparel was "xx tymes more in value than it was an c yere ago."[30] This demand for a more "abundant material life" naturally stimulated both commerce and industry.

Another cause, a reversal of one of the principal causes for the decline, was first the recovery and then the increased consolidation of the western European states. Following the termination of the Hundred Years' War, France began to recover politically and to rebuild her economy. The revived monarchy encouraged the expansion of industry, commerce, finance, and transportation;[31] the public responded; and within four decades the country was sufficiently recovered to venture on territorial expansion beyond its frontiers. In the first century of the Renaissance period wars involving France were fought on French soil; after 1494 they were waged abroad, on Italian soil or on the frontiers and not in the heart of the country. The shift is a clear measure of French economic recovery. The Spanish "Century of Troubles" was followed by the era of Ferdinand and Isabella, a brilliant era of political consolidation and territorial expansion. As in France this political recovery resulted in an upsurge of commerce and industry. In England the Wars of the Roses were followed by the Tudors who consolidated the monarchy, restored order, and promoted commerce and industry. To be sure this political recovery was not universal. Italy was being disturbed by the imperial wars of France and Spain; the Venetian empire was being truncated by the Turks; Germany was suffering from the destructive peasants' revolts; Scandinavia was bleeding from repeated rebellions against the Union of Calmar; Prussia and Poland were being ravaged by the wars between the Poles and the Teutonic Knights; and Hungary and the Balkans were being harried by repeated Turkish onslaughts. Yet, when the balance is struck, the recovery of the west seems to have been substantial enough to assure an over-all increase in commerce.

Stimulating the recovery further was the introduction of new industries, new in the literal sense or new in the sense that now they became widespread in contrast to their localized existence before. Printing, cannon casting, and gunpowder making may be cited as totally new industries. They appeared in this period and spread quickly throughout the continent. Silkmaking, glassmaking, and paper making may be cited as examples of the latter type. They were extant before, in the later Middle Ages, but for the most part only in Italy. Now they were being introduced into most European countries. Whether belonging to the first category or to the second, these new industries added substantially to the volume of commerce in the second period.

Finally, the discovery of new lands beyond the seas must be included as a factor also. While the opening of these new lands did not have a revolutionary effect on Renaissance commerce, it was not without influence on the volume of commerce during the late Renaissance. The expansion of shipbuilding alone, required by this overseas program, was bound to produce an increase. Also there was an increase in the trade of such tropical commodities as negro slaves,[32] ivory, sugar, and medicinal herbs. Sugar, for example, once just a trickle from Sicily, in 1493 reached the astounding production of 120,000 *arrobas* a year in the island of Madeira alone, of which a third was just for the Flanders market.[33]

Such then is the over-all picture of the volume of commerce during the Renaissance — a serious decline in the first century of the period followed by a slow recovery which picked up tempo as the Renaissance came to the close. The net gain, however — and this is of capital importance — was not of such magnitude as to produce a revolution in Renaissance economy as tradition represents.

Institutions of Commerce

CRAFT SHOP One agency engaged in the selling of goods was the agency which made the goods, that is, the craft shop. The hatters, the glovers, the cobblers, the coopers, the wheelwrights, and the various other specialists made their respective articles and sold them. However, they only sold a part of their output on their premises. The public and the authorities were not yet receptive to the principle of free trade, that is, to the notion of trading in daily necessities in private shops. Such trading, it was felt, did not lend itself to ready supervision. They preferred to see marketing done in public under the watchful eyes of the Clerk of the Market and his duly appointed assistants. This could be best done on the market.

MARKETS Markets were places where the people of the community, peasants from the manors and townsmen, assembled to sell their products and to buy their needs. Peasants brought their produce of the land, their fowl, and their dairy products; craftsmen, the wares of their shops; and both sold and bought as their needs dictated. In large towns there were separate markets, one for grain, another for fish, a third for meat, and still others for cloth and other commodities. They were located in different quarters of the town and were held on different days. All were carefully regulated in the interest of fair dealing and very frequently in the interest of the local, as against "foreign," traders. They were truly indispensable to the welfare of the community, for, together with the craft shop, the local bakery, and the local ale house, they provided the people with their main needs.

ENTREPRENEURS Important as the craftsmen were as distributors of goods, they naturally were unable to meet all the demands of the consumers and of the business world. The bakers of Barcelona might sell their loaves of bread, but to do so they had to depend on grain brought to the city. True, some of it might be provided by the peasant cultivators of the district, but in time the local output would be exhausted. Hence grain would have to be imported from more distant regions, as for example in 1347, when by arrangement with the city authorities some 200,000 bushels were brought in.[34] Naturally this would give rise to grain dealers. The same would apply to such other commodities as wool, cloth, spices, salt, or iron. Obviously, then, there was need for some middlemen who would obtain the necessary commodities wherever these were to be found and resell them to the public; that is, there was need for professional merchants or entrepreneurs as they are often called.

These middlemen appeared early in the Middle Ages. Some of them emerged from the more enterprising peddlers, like the famous St. Godric;[35] and some, probably the great majority, from the more resourceful craftsmen. They grew in number and inportance as commerce expanded from the eleventh century on, and to protect their interests they formed themselves, like the craftsmen, into gilds and frequently secured controlling influence in their municipal governments. During the Renaissance they maintained their position and continued to perform their special roles as dealers in commodities which were not of local provenience.[36]

CRAFTSMEN-ENTREPRENEURS So far the entrepreneur and the craftsman who sold his own product have been presented as distinct operators. Indeed, their functions being different, these businessmen as a rule were separate individuals. But in many cases the entrepreneur and the craftsman were one and the same person. The Fuggers were entrepreneurs, but in their initial stages they were actually weavers; so were the Medici; so were the Marcels of Paris; and so were hundreds of others through-

out the continent. Sometimes it was the dyer who turned middleman
without ceasing to be a dyer. Thus, for example, some dyers of Leicester,
as early as the middle of the thirteenth century, were entrepreneurs

> . . . purchasing wool, having it washed and dyed in blue, vermilion
> or other colors, probably on their own premises, giving it out to carders
> and spinners, employing weavers and fullers throughout the town,
> under stringent supervision, at piece-work rates fixed by themselves,
> and marketing the finished cloth from their own stalls at the great
> East Anglian Fairs of Boston, St. Ives or Stamford.[37]

Similar examples of this duality of roles might be cited from other
than cloth trades. There were merchant cutlers who manufactured cut-
lery in their own shops and who dealt wholesale in imported ivory and
fine steel; there were cordwainers who dealt in alum leather; and gold-
smiths who sold imported metallic thread; and many more. Often
enough these middlemen-artisans provoked bitter opposition on the
part of the simple craftsmen, and municipal laws were passed restrain-
ing the overly zealous entrepreneurs from engrossing the merchandising
activities for themselves. But craft industry and trade being so intimately allied, it was really impossible to stop the practice, and so these
men of dual roles continued to hold their place as merchandisers.

FAIRS The Leicester dyer, we are told, was found marketing his
cloth at the fairs of Boston, St. Ives, and Stamford. Apparently he had
more cloth than could be profitably disposed of on the local markets
and so he took it to places where greater quantities of goods could be
sold, namely, to the great fairs. Fairs, then, were as necessary for the
entrepreneurs as markets were to the local craftsmen and vice versa.

From these few remarks the nature of the fairs can be deduced.
They were, it is clear, "periodical meeting-places for professional merchants" who bought and sold goods in substantial quantities.[38] They
were authorized by territorial authorities and so were found only in
specific places. While many towns were allowed to operate them, some,
especially the large cities where international trade was a year-round
affair, such as Venice and Milan, did not have large-scale fairs.

Being substantial undertakings, fairs were held only from one to four
times a year, but they usually lasted several days, or even weeks, at a
time. Normally, also, definite days were designated for transactions in

specific commodities, and a period was set aside at the end of the fair to enable dealers to make their payments and to balance their accounts.

To promote a large concourse of merchants at these fairs, the authorities provided conveniences and protection and extended valuable privileges. They had display stalls erected and available for rent; they licensed money-changers to facilitate transactions between merchants of different lands; and in general they tried to assure efficiency of operations and to maintain peace and order. Among the privileges which they extended were safe conduct, exemption from "repraisals for crimes committed or debts contracted outside" the fair, suspension of lawsuits against merchants for the duration of "the peace of the fair," and "suspension of the canonical prohibition of usury." In a word, everything was done to make the fair a business success, both for the patron who wanted his coffers filled with revenue from rents and licenses and for the merchants who wanted to transact as great a volume of business as possible.

Though not as numerous as markets, the fairs were quite plentiful. All countries had them, and through them commodities from all of Europe and, indeed, from the known world were distributed. Hence, what the markets were to the communities, the fairs were to the regions and the states; and the entrepreneur made all this possible.

Fairs like markets date from far back in the Middle Ages. They multiplied with the general expansion of business. Of course, some declined as commerce shifted to some different route or business methods changed. The Champagne fairs, for example, were undoubtedly the most important fairs in Europe in the thirteenth century, but toward the end of the century, as the cloth industry of northern Italy surpassed that of Flanders, and Italian merchants began to transport their wares by sea around Spain and to bring them directly to Bruges or Southampton,[39] the *raison d'être* of the fairs disappeared and the fairs declined. Some fairs withered, if they did not disappear, when wholesalers established permanent warehouses and retailers came to them to obtain their needs. But while admittedly some fairs disappeared or declined during the Renaissance, the institution had not yet reached its end. Many old fairs were still thriving, as in the case of Lille and Ypres or in the case of Chiavari and Sestre in northern Italy; while others showing signs of decline had fresh life breathed into them by the governments, as in the case of the fairs of Lyon, or were replaced by younger and more active ones, as in the case of Geneva, Bruges, Antwerp, Frankfurt-on-Main, Leipzig, and Scania in Denmark. Moreover, new fairs were actually founded, such as that of Bergen op Zoom about 1350,[40] Malines in 1409, Medina del Campo sometime between 1406 and 1412, Ghent in 1455, Clermont-Ferrand and Rouen in the reign of Louis XI, and Courtrai in 1531. Hence, though there were definite signs of decline and of possible supersession, the Renaissance fairs continued to serve as vital institutions of commerce.

COMPANIES: THREE GENERAL TYPES While some individual entrepreneurs had enough capital to engage in large-scale business, there were scores of others who lacked sufficient capital and found it necessary to pool their resources. There were also men with money who for one reason or another could not personally manage an enterprise; and on the other hand there were those with merchandising experience but no capital. In either case the logical solution was for the people concerned to enter into a business association. Thus companies came into being — another important business institution during the Renaissance period.

There were three general types of companies: the partnership, the regulated company, and the joint-stock company.

PARTNERSHIPS Partnerships varied in composition. One type consisted of one or more providers of capital, which could consist of money, goods, or instruments of production, and a factor (manager) who provided his services and, in some instances, a little capital. The association was of short duration, often only for the completion of the transaction, and profits were prorated. In 1437, for example, Antoine Latin and Bernard del Olm, both of Toulouse, joined in a partnership for a year, Antoine providing cloth valued at 40 *moutons* of gold and a mule, and Bernard 7 *moutons* in coin and service. The latter was to drive the mule, visit the fairs, and sell and buy. Antoine was to get two-thirds of the profit and Bernard one-third.[41] Such an association was called *commenda.*

Another type of partnership was an association of two or three members each of whom provided some capital and participated in the operations. Generally, such a partnership did not dissolve after each transaction, but lasted longer — two, or three, or even several years. Profits were divided on a prearranged ratio depending on the size and nature of each partner's contribution to the enterprise, and audits were made semiannually or more frequently. Such a partnership was known as a *compagnia*. If the partners were members of the same family, the partnership naturally was a family partnership. This differed in at least two ways from the two preceding types. For one thing, it had a longer life. Whereas the *commenda* and the *compagnia* normally lasted for the duration of each venture, or at most from three to seven years, the family partnerships lasted for life or even for more than one generation. Secondly, and because of its longer life, the family partnership permitted the undertaking of several different ventures at the same time and the creation of subsidiary associations. Common in many cities, and represented by such famous associations as that of the Medici and the Fuggers, the family partnerships were particularly prominent in Genoa, Tuscany, and Venice.[42]

A good illustration of these family companies is that of the Alberti of Florence.[43] The first known partnership of this family dates back to 1302 when the three sons of Jacopo degli Alberti, Alberto, Neri, and Lapo, pooled their resources to engage in cloth trade between Florence and Flanders via the Champagne fairs. It is not clear what funds each member contributed to the company at its inception, but in 1323, when the firm was revamped to include the sons of the founders, the base capital was £25,000 *affiorino* of which Alberto and his three sons had eleven shares, Neri four, and Lapo's two sons, ten. In addition, some members had investments beyond the base capital, Alberto having approximately £2,140, his son Jacopo about £1,820, and Lapo's two sons, close to £2,360. Books were to be closed every second year, and profits were to be prorated according to each member's share of the base capital. For the extra capital invested, the return was 8 per cent; on the other hand, members paid 8 per cent penalty if their actual investment fell below their base share, that is, 8 per cent interest on the deficit.

With only some minor departures from the structure established in 1323, the company continued for twenty years under the able leadership of Alberto, and then under Neri's son Agnolo. But when Agnolo retired in 1343, the firm began to splinter, first, by 1347, into two competing firms, Alberti "antichi" and Alberti "nouvi," and then into additional branches, so that by 1400 there were several distinct Alberti family concerns in Florence, Bruges, and Barcelona.

At first, until the end of the 1320's, the firm engaged in trade with Flanders, purchasing finished cloth and selling it throughout Italy. Then, as Florence developed its woolen industry, they bought "raw" cloth, finished it, apparently in their own shops, and retailed it. To expedite the transactions the firm employed traveling agents and permanent correspondents. In 1307, for example, they had traveling representatives in Champagne and Flanders, and resident factors in Barletta, Bologna, Milan, Naples, and Venice, a total of fourteen men. In 1348, the Champagne fairs having declined in the meantime, the traveling agents disappeared, and only permanent agents remained, in Avignon, Naples, and Barletta; but toward the end of the fourteenth century the Alberti "antichi," who had become papal bankers in the meantime, maintained branches in Avignon, Barcelona, Barletta, Bologna, Bruges, Genoa, Naples, London, Paris, Perugia, and Venice.

Some idea of the volume of business which the original partnership transacted can be obtained from the fiscal statement for the two-year period, November 1323 to November 1325. Their total investment during these two years, including the £25,000 *affiorino* of initial capital, was £34,513. 11s. 7d., and their profits amounted to £8,187. 5s. 6d. These are substantial figures, not much smaller, as will appear in the chapter on finance, than those employed by the Medici, one of the greatest merchant families of the Renaissance period proper.

In Germany, especially in the Hanseatic trade, there was an additional type of partnership, the mutual agency partnership (*gegenseitige Ferngesellschaft*).[44] This was a loose-working arrangement between two merchants in different cities agreeing to sell each other's consignments. There was neither common capital nor common accounting. The partners relied on each other's integrity and struck balances irregularly, at times only after several years, as in the case of the Reval and Lubeck partners who engaged in selling each other's goods for seventeen years (1507–1523) before making a settlement.

RegULATED COMPANY The regulated company was a company chartered by public authorities and consisted of a large group of venturesome merchants trading in the same general area. It was simply a company of merchants and not of capital. Each merchant brought his goods to the port of loading, transported his goods in ships leased by the company at a charge fixed by the company, stored his wares in company warehouses, sold them at a price fixed by the company, invested the money from the sales in new purchases at prices regulated by the company, brought them back to the point of origin, and sold them on the home market. After such a voyage a member might withdraw, but the company continued. The distinguishing feature of this type of company was that it had no pooling of capital and no sharing of profits, and the main reasons for its existence were that it regulated the trade of its individual members for the advantage of all and that it brought them greater prestige in a foreign land and greater security for their goods and persons both on the high seas and on the foreign markets. This is exemplified in the case of the Andalusia Company. English merchants had been trading in southern Spain, with their headquarters in the port of San Lucar de Barrameda, as early as the thirteenth century. Their trade was welcome, and privileges were extended to them by the lords of the region. Naturally the resident merchants must have had frequent occasions for cooperating with each other, but there was no official union until they were incorporated by Henry VIII's charter in 1530, in order to strengthen their position in the face of rising discrimination at the hands of Spanish authorities when relations between England and Spain began to deteriorate.[45] Perhaps another reason was the steady decrease, in the fourteenth century, in the number of great individual capitalists, due mostly to the bankruptcies of their royal borrowers, and a corresponding increase in the number of middling traders. Whereas before that time the merchant-financiers had enough private capital to operate competitively, the small exporters who succeeded them found competition too risky and so sought security in regulation. Furthermore, this increase in the number of smaller merchants was taking place at the very time when the continental market, for reasons stated above, was actually contracting. Cartels and regulation became therefore even more desirable, hence the emergence of the regulated company.

One of the most famous of such companies was the Company of Merchant Adventurers in England.[46] It was long in developing. At an undetermined date in the Middle Ages London merchant gildsmen trading in Europe, but mostly in the Netherlands, began to get together to discuss their common problems and to coordinate their efforts. Out of such assemblies emerged recognized associations or Fellowships as they called themselves. There were several of them at first, that of the Mercers, Drapers, Haberdashers, Grocers, and others, and they managed their affairs independently of each other. In time, all the London Fellowships began to consult with each other. To defend their interests abroad and to represent their case to their own government they found it advantageous to act in common, and so a slow fusion commenced, with the influential Fellowship of Mercers serving as a unifying core. This natural but slow consolidation was quickened in the fifteenth century by the actions of the crown when it was called upon to settle several international crises in which English trade and traders were involved. To resolve the difficulties the English kings found it desirable to treat the interests of the various Fellowships in common. Instead of addressing themselves to the Fellowships severally, they began to communicate with them through the mayor of London, and this naturally led to the election of representatives who could speak for all the Fellowships. Thus the interests of the crown and of the merchants coincided, and in the end, in 1486, when Henry VII needed the unity of all the merchants trading in the Low Countries in order to employ effective economic pressures in his diplomatic maneuvering, the Company of Merchant Adventurers was officially born. At first it comprised only the London Fellowships, but shortly thereafter by royal directive the Fellowships of the other towns were incorporated and the Company became national in scope, though it was the London group that dominated and guided it. Thus consolidated, the Company became the greatest commercial organization in Tudor England.

To manage its affairs the Company elected a governor and a court of twenty-four assistants. This governing body had the right to make regulations, subject to the approval of the members assembled in a court. It was empowered to try cases of noncompliance and interloping, to assess penalties, and to enforce its decisions. It negotiated with foreign governments; planned the shipping, convoying if necessary, and marketing; regulated prices; passed on the costs of transportation; and handled the company funds. To assist the governing board with the routine of administration there were several subordinate officers: a clerk who acted as a corresponding secretary, a treasurer and auditors, "appointers" who supervised the preparation of the transport fleet, and "conduitors" who computed and assessed the costs of transportation. With such an administration to govern the overeas ventures of its members, the Company of Merchant Adventurers was truly "regulated."

JOINT-STOCK COMPANY The third type, namely the joint-stock company, was a company of capital. Individuals interested bought stock in a company which had a regular board of elected directors who managed the capital in buying, transporting, and selling goods, and in declaring profits and losses. The significance of this type of company for commerce was that it permitted the concentration of vast sums of money in one project and made possible ventures much larger than could be undertaken by individual merchants or even partnerships. Thus one of the first joint-stock companies, the Muscovy Company, which was founded in 1553 with 240 shares of £25 sterling each, in ten years built up a capital of £336,000. It could hope therefore to penetrate, in quest of business, into the very depths of distant Russia. Another advantage which the joint-stock company offered was its permanence. Shareholders might die, but their shares, whether retained by the heirs or sold outside the family, remained intact; and the company suffered no disruption. Finally, the joint-stock company, barring some exceptions in the early days of its history, offered its members the boon of limited liability. Whereas the *compagnia* and the family partnership in the event of failure carried with them the threat of unlimited liability whereby each partner was held liable for all the debts of the concern, the joint-stock company's principle of limited liability made each stockholder liable only in the amount equal to the funds which he invested in the firm.

One would expect that with all these advantages the joint-stock form of organization would readily supplant the older forms of organization. The fact is, however, that during the Renaissance the joint-stock company was quite an uncertain and hesitating fledgling. The

Muscovy Company which had started as a joint-stock venture converted into a regulated company in 1622. The English East India Company, organized in 1600, did likewise between 1698 and 1708; and in its initial years it often struck balances after each voyage and divided up the capital and the profit, in reality therefore limiting its life only to a single venture. Limited liability, perhaps the greatest boon that the joint-stock company could offer to the business world, was slow in coming during the Renaissance and did not become universally recognized until the nineteenth century. Lastly, and perhaps because of these uncertainties, the number of such companies during the Renaissance was small; and of these some limited their operations to overseas trade with the newly discovered lands and therefore only to a small percentage of the total volume of commerce.

"MIXED"-TYPE COMPANIES In an age which saw the evolution of various types of business organizations on a trial-and-error basis, so to speak, types could not be pure. We have just seen, for example, that the East India Company after starting as a joint-stock company changed to the regulated type and then back to its original form. We should expect, therefore, some hybrid or "mixed" types.

One example which combined the family-partnership type of organization with that of the joint-stock company was the Maona of Chios. This was an association of Genoese shipping magnates and capitalists who in return for helping Genoa reconquer Chios (1346) — in 1304 Chios had been ceded as a fief to Benedetto Zaccharia, a Genoese merchant and seaman, by emperor Andronicus II, but it was retaken by the Byzantines in 1329 — were given the right, for an annual fee of 2,500 *lire,* to administer the island and its dependencies and to exploit their economy. The association sold shares in the company, but while these shares were negotiable, they apparently did not pass outside the families of the founders. The association had a council and a governor who made policy and actually governed the island. The members held together so closely that after 1362, when the association was reorganized, they took the name *Guistiniani* after the name of its headquarters in Chios, the Palazzo Guistiniani.

Another example, somewhere between the regulated and the joint-stock company were the Genoese *Societies* organized to deal in one commodity, such as mercury, salt, coral, alum. Of these the most highly developed was the *Society of Alum* which was organized in 1449. This was a company of men each of whom had proprietary rights to certain amounts of alum — Francesco Draperio, for example, having an interest in 250,000 cantares (about 12,900 tons), Pietro Paterio in 33,570, Baldasare Adorno in 36,660, and so forth. Some of these members, in turn, had subsidiary societies, that is, partners who owned parts of the principal member's stock, which parts, like shares in a stock company, were transferable. The Society had unsalaried, elected officers to serve as managers of the entire operation. These in turn were advised by a Council of Administration; and since the organization had international dealings, it maintained local representatives in various centers. Each member of the Society contributed to the cost of operations in proportion to his holding and shared in its profits on the same basis, and all were responsible for the Society's obligations. In some respects, then, the Society was like a regulated company and in others like a joint-stock company.[47]

HANSEATIC LEAGUE Not a company but an organization designed to promote trade in northern Europe was the Hanseatic League. The League came into being shortly after 1282 when a number of associations of German towns joined in one comprehensive organization. Among these regional unions were (1) the Lubeck-Hamburg-Bremen group, (2) the Cologne group, (3) the London association, (4) the association of Novgorod, and (5) the Bruges group. Each of these had been evolving during the century from 1150 to 1250 and establishing crisscross commercial bonds with one another; and when the network of these ties webbed them all into a firm economic group, the League came into being.

The purpose for the regional unions was primarily defense against attacks of robber barons on the land and river routes and of pirates on the seas; while the reason for the fusion into one League was not only the need for protection, which always remained an impelling motive, but a desire to secure monopoly of trade in the Baltic and in the eastern part of the North Sea. By pooling their resources and coordinating their policies the members felt that they could obtain advantageous trading concessions in England, Scandinavia, and in the eastern

Baltic lands, suppress piracy, and eject interlopers who should dare to invade their preserve. In these objectives they had great success. From the Steelyard in London to their *kontor* in Novgorod, Russia, their ships controlled the waters throughout the fourteenth and fifteenth centuries. The extent of the League's power and success can be measured by the terms of the Treaty of Stralsund which they imposed on the Danish king Waldemar IV, in May, 1370, after defeating him in a war provoked by his raid on the League town of Wisby and by his general anti-League policies. For the treaty conceded to them not only freedom of navigation in the straits between Denmark and Scania, exemption from customs duties, the right to establish and maintain branches in Danish territory, and occupation of several Danish cities for five years as an indemnity, but also the right to be consulted about the succession to the throne. The League's power was not to be disputed.

Administratively the League, comprising between seventy to eighty towns, was organized into a number of divisions called circles. The Wendish circle, with Lubeck as its center, included the towns in the territories of Mecklenburg and Pomerania. Farther to the east and encompassing the lands of the Teutonic Knights was the Livonian circle, with its capital at Danzig. The third division was the Saxon circle, which embraced such old towns as Goslar, Hanover, Halle, Bremen, Magdeburg, and Hildesheim, and had Brunswick as its center. The last to be created, in the year 1367, with Cologne as its chief post, was the Westphalian circle which took in Westphalia, the lower Rhineland, and the Netherlands. These local unions were subject to the authority of the officers and diet elected by the entire League whose capital was the enterprising city of Lubeck. Thus the organization possessed both flexibility and centralization.

The merchants of the League were primarily middlemen. They traded Baltic herring, timber, tar, pitch, wax, fur, hemp, Prussian wheat, and Swedish copper and iron for English wool and cloth, Flemish textiles, Brabantine metalware, French wines and salt, German fustian, silver, and salt, Italian silks and velvets, and oriental spices and other luxury goods which the Italians brought to Bruges, a great trading center in the west where the League maintained a thriving *kontor*. But their main commodity — staple it may be called — was salted herring. The spawning area of the herring in the fourteenth and fifteenth centuries was the waters south of Sweden. The catch was rich, the packing cheap because of the accessibility to abundant supplies of timber for barrels, the market close by, and the demand extensive. Profits were substantial and the League throve.

The height of the League's prosperity seems to have come in the first quarter of the fifteenth century. Thereafter successive troubles began to beset the League and, as these multiplied cumulatively, decline naturally set in.[48]

Among these troubles two were crucial. One was the shift of the herring from the waters of the Sound to the North Sea. As long as the herring homed in the waters east of Denmark, Lubeck and its companion Baltic towns had a near-monopoly on the herring trade and so a commanding hold on the League towns which depended on this trade. In the early fifteenth century, for some unknown reason, the herring shifted to the waters of the North Sea. This deprived Lubeck of its advantageous position and invited the Hollanders and the North Sea towns of Bremen and Hamburg to expand their fishing industry and to enter the international herring trade on their own. For Lubeck this meant a substantial drop in its business, and for Bremen and Hamburg this meant that membership in the League was no longer indispensable. The other trouble was a chance combination of several derangements in the commerce of northern Europe. Until the close of the fifteenth century the region from the Seine to the lower Elbe had been able to procure its grain supplies locally and from southern England. This generally kept the traders of this region out of the Baltic waters and made Lubeck's services as intermediary necessary. But when these sources proved to be inadequate and grain had to be imported from the Baltic states, shippers and dealers from the North Sea ports began to invade the Baltic waters in ever-increasing numbers and weakened Lubeck's primacy. Their invasion grew when the salt deposits of Luneberg, controlled by Lubeck and hitherto depended upon by the Baltic lands, began to run out and salt had to be imported from the French salt works of Bourgneuf on the Bay of Biscay, for thereafter the shippers were assured of cargos both ways, salt from the west and grain from the Baltic. It increased still more when their shipping needs neces-

sitated the importation of lumber which they found available in the
Baltic lands. Finally, since the bulkiness of grain, salt, and lumber made
their transshipments difficult and expensive and prohibitive, traders
in these commodities began to use the all-sea route around the peninsula
of Denmark in preference to the hitherto customary sea and land route
across Holstein. Since the land portage began at Lubeck, the by-passing
of this route naturally hurt Lubeck both in profits and in influence. As
all these derangements developed concurrently, Lubeck's privileged
position steadily deteriorated and the League itself became dispensable.

Supplementing these major troubles was a host of lesser adversities.
The English, who were practically barred from the Baltic from the
middle of the fifteenth century, revived their competition a century
later. They forced the Hansa to readmit them into the Baltic waters,
and when this readmission turned out to be futile, they opened the
White Sea route to Russia, thereby by-passing the Hansa traders as
middlemen; they revoked the League's preferential treatment in England; and finally, in 1598, they closed its famous London depot, the
Steelyard. The Russians annexed Novgorod and soon expelled the
League from this its easternmost trading center. Sweden became independent and strong under Gustavus Vasa and challenged Hansa's exploitation. Finally, the principal Hansa entrepot in the west, Bruges,
declined.

With all these adverse factors operating simultaneously, the League's
days were numbered, though it was not until a century later that the
League ceased to be anything but a name.

While these were the types of commercial organizations which prevailed during the Renaissance, it is not to be assumed that they were
associated with this age alone. The *commenda* and the partnerships
were widely used in the Middle Ages and continued into the Renaissance period practically unchanged. The regulated companies developed
in the Middle Ages but they played their great role during the Renaissance and so may be regarded as a Renaissance institution. The joint-
stock company, despite some antecedents in the Middle Ages, was really
a child of the Renaissance. But, born late in the Renaissance, it remained an infant until the seventeenth century and so played a minor
role in Renaissance commerce. On the other hand, the Hansa originated

in the Middle Ages, attained its full development by the time of the Renaissance, and fought a slow, losing battle during the latter half of the age. Hence if any type is to be identified specifically with the Renaissance age, it would appear to be the regulated company.

Instruments and Techniques of Commerce

Turning from commercial agencies to some business instruments and techniques, we find that the two most important instruments during the Renaissance were deposit transfers and bills of exchange, while the most significant technique was the double-entry bookkeeping. Insurance may also be included here.

DEPOSIT TRANSFERS Deposit transfers were one means of making payments for purchases without the actual transfer of specie from one person to another. Having negotiated a transaction, the parties concerned, or their authorized agents, would proceed to a money-changer or to a banker with whom the buyer had an account and the buyer would request that an amount equal to the value of the purchase be transferred from his deposit account to the account of the seller. The banker would simply make the necessary entries in his books and the deal would be considered closed. No money changed hands. This method was used extensively during the Renaissance, but it dates far back in the Middle Ages and was in wide use at the medieval Champagne fairs. In fact, the regulations of the fairs provided several days at the end of each fair for such "clearing-house" operations. This system is therefore medieval as well as Renaissance.

THE BILL OF EXCHANGE The bill of exchange[49] was also a means of making payments without the transfer of money, but whereas the method of deposit transfers could be used only when the two parties were in the same place, the bill of exchange could be used to meet obligations between parties in two separate and distant places. A merchant of Bruges having to pay a merchant of Florence for a shipment of silk would go to a banker of Bruges with connections in Florence and buy from him with the specie of Bruges at an agreed rate of exchange and in the amount of his obligation a bill drawn on the banker's agent in Florence and payable to the silk merchant. The bill would have to be delivered to the Florentine merchant and presented to the banker's agent for payment within a definite time limit of thirty, forty, or sixty days, depending on the distance between the place of issue and the place of payment, known as usance. The bill having been presented and paid, the deal would be closed; and yet no bullion need be transferred from Bruges to Florence.

In addition to the aforementioned bill of exchange there was a variant type which was used to provide credit. For example, X of Bruges needs money to buy goods to send to his agent X_1 in Barcelona to be sold there. He secures the money from Y in Bruges, but the loan is disguised as a purchase of exchange, that is, of Barcelona money for "value received." With the money advanced, X purchases the goods and dispatches them to his agent. At the same time he sends to his agent a request — the bill of exchange — directing him to pay Y's agent in Barcelona the amount stipulated in the bill and in money of Barcelona. On receipt of the bill his agent (X_1) pays the amount to Y's agent, and reimburses himself from the sale of the goods. By this device then X got a short-term loan for the duration of the period stipulated in the letter and employed it in merchandising, from which he and his agent hoped to make a profit. But what did Y get? In the first place, he charged a fee for the service and also for the risk involved. In the second place, although this fact did not appear on the bill, he usually advanced less than the face value of the bill, the difference being tantamount to interest collected in advance. In addition, he might profit from fluctuations in exchange rates, though of course he ran the risk of loss as well. Both parties therefore could hope for some profit. Moreover, this device circumvented the church's ban on usury, for on the surface the transaction appeared to be a purchase of foreign exchange at one place and payable at another which the church permitted as valid. Hence, regarded as bona fide and at the same time serving the "buyer" and the "seller" in a useful and profitable way, the bill of exchange came to be used very extensively.

While used widely during the Renaissance, the bill of exchange appeared in Italy in the thirteenth century and spread rapidly in the Mediterranean area and France wherever Italian merchants were engaged in business. England and Germany, however, did not adopt it until the Renaissance period proper.

Like many other things, the bill of exchange did not appear fully developed at the time of its inception. It had an antecedent, the widely used medieval notarial contract. X, needing money with which to buy goods to be taken to the Champagne fairs, secured the necessary money from Y. They both proceeded to a notary who drew up an instrument by which X bound himself to pay Y in money of Champagne at some Champagne fair, or, failing that, to pay him in money at the place of issuance. The sum payable at the Champagne fair was usually greater than that advanced, and that payable at the point of origin was still greater. In that way X secured a loan to employ in merchandising and Y was assured of some profit. The resemblance between this transaction and that connected with the bill of exchange is close enough to warrant the conclusion that the latter derived from the former.[50] Since one of the differences was that the borrower in the case of the notarial contract traveled with the goods, whereas in the case of the bill of exchange he worked through an agent, some economic historians are of the opinion that the bill of exchange came into being when the itinerant merchant was replaced by the sedentary merchant, which change they attribute to the decline of the Champagne fairs and the rise of Bruges as the new northern European commercial entrepot.[51]

INSURANCE The extensiveness of maritime commerce in the later Middle Ages and the hazards that beset it led in time to the development of insurance.[52]

An early form of insurance resulted from an arrangement between a merchant who contributed capital, money or goods, to an overseas venture and the merchant who conducted the venture. Experience taught that under normal circumstances the contributor might expect to realize 6 to 8 per cent on his contribution. However, if he were a cautious type he might prefer security with less profit: he might arrange to forego half his share of the profit in favor of the conductor on condition that the latter guarantee to return the full value of the contribution. It is clear that such a contract was really in the nature of insurance. Since in one sense the transaction was also a loan — the contributor advancing capital to the conductor which the latter used to increase the cargo — but a loan which circumvented the principle of usury because the profit was not fixed, it steadily gained in usage.

Another form of insurance appeared in Genoa about the middle of the fourteenth century under the guise of a contract of purchase and sale. The insurer was represented as a buyer who agreed to buy a cargo in question only in the event it did *not* reach its destination safely; and for this offer to purchase, the owner of the cargo, that is, the insured, paid a service charge, or what is now called a premium.[53]

The next step was direct premium insurance without any disguise; and this, too, appeared about the middle of the fourteenth century. Thus, for example, in consideration of a premium of 54 florins one Leonardo Cataneo, a merchant of Genoa, insured a cargo of wheat worth 300 florins to be shipped from Sciacca in Sicily to Tunis.[54] Again, for a premium of 8 gold florins Francesco of Prato and his partners, doing business in Pisa, insured for 200 gold florins a cargo of cloth which the trader Ambrogio was shipping from Porto Pisano to Palermo in a ship belonging to a certain Bartolomeo Vitale.[55] This, of course, is direct insurance, and it too grew in usage.

How extensively insurance was sold during the Renaissance period can be seen from some extant business records. Thus the journal of Giovanni Piccamiglio, a Genoese merchant of only moderate means, shows that in the period from 1456 to 1459 he underwrote thirty-nine insurance contracts for a total of 6,607 *lire*.[56] Thus the account books of Bernardo Cambi, a Florentine merchant who did business in Bruges from 1435 to 1450 and thereafter in Florence, show that between 1442 and 1477 he insured fifty-seven vessels sailing between various ports all the way from Constantinople to Southampton and Sluys.[57] There were many other insurers like Piccamiglio and Cambi, and there also were agents who merely wrote business in behalf of underwriting firms. On the whole, one gets the impression from the evidence available that the insurance business which had appeared in the thirteenth century in the ports of the Mediterranean became quite common throughout western Europe during the Renaissance. It should be pointed out, however, that in the Hansa territory, which in business techniques was at least a century behind the Mediterranean basin, the first known example of insurance appears in 1531, and that is quite late in the Renaissance.

DOUBLE-ENTRY BOOKKEEPING   Double-entry bookkeeping is regarded by businessmen as an indispensable method of keeping themselves posted on their financial standing, and its adoption has been interpreted as a sign of commercial maturity. It was first used in Genoa sometime between 1278 and 1340. Thence it spread into Tuscany where it became an established system by the 1380's. It appeared in Venice by 1406, and before the end of the century it was in use throughout most of Italy.[58] Helping to popularize it and to carry it beyond the Alps was the treatise which Luca Paccioli prepared on it in 1494 and included in his work on mathematics — *Summa de arithmetica, geometri, proportioni et proportionalita.*[59] About the same time the Fugger firm carried it into Germany from their branch office in Venice. By 1518 they were employing it in their headquarters at Augsburg, as is evidenced by a "set of model books" prepared by one of their bookkeepers, Matthaus Schwarz, who had spent some time in Italy learning Italian business methods.[60] Undoubtedly the method was adopted throughout their branches in Germany, and from there, in the course of the century, it passed into widespread use. Like the bill of exchange and insurance, then, double-entry bookkeeping came into wide use during the Renaissance. But whereas the bill of exchange and insurance were already quite common in the Middle Ages, double-entry bookkeeping, despite its appearance in the late 1200's, was really a Renaissance development. The Alberti books, for example, although covering the period 1302 to 1348, were not yet drawn up in accordance with this new system of bookkeeping.[61] Indeed, treatises on single-entry bookkeeping were still being published in Germany as late as 1518.[62]

1. On this trade see Jacques Heers, *Gênes au xve siècle,* 321–50, table XV and the corresponding map.
2. Y. Renouard, "Le grand commerce des vins de Gascogne au moyen âge," *Revue historique,* CCXXI (1959), 261–304; Roger Dion, "Le commerce des vins de Beauné au moyen âge," *Revue historique,* CCXIV (1955), 209–21.
3. For a penetrating account of this trade see Raymond de Roover, "La balance commerciale entre les Pays-Bas et l'Italie au quinzième siècle," *RB,* XXXVII (1959), 374–86; M. E. Mallett, "Anglo-Florentine Commercial Relations, 1465–1491," *EcHR,* 2d series, XV (1962), 250–65; and W. B. Watson, "The Structure of the Florentine Galley Trade

54 ECONOMY AND SOCIETY

with Flanders and England in the Fifteenth Century," *RB*, XXXIX (1961), 1073–91, and XL (1962), 317–47. Watson's article supplements and corrects De Roover's study.

4. An extremely valuable account of the streams and their webbing is to be found in Heer's study of fifteenth-century Genoa (*op. cit., passim,* but especially, 416–98, tables XVII–XIX, XXI, and the maps at the end of the book); in Domenico Gioffré, *Gênes et les foires de change de Lyon à Besançon, École pratique des hautes études* — VIᵉ section, *Centre de recherches historiques, Affaires et gens d'affaires,* XXI (Paris: S.E.V.P.E.N., 1960), 25–87; and in Mollat *et al., op. cit.,* 737–46.

5. For some literature on medieval commerce see the following: *CEcH*, vol. II, *Trade and Industry in the Middle Ages* (Cambridge: Cambridge University Press, 1952), chaps. iv and v especially; Henri Pirenne, *Economic and Social History of Medieval Europe,* trans. I. E. Clegg (New York: Harcourt, Brace and Co., 1937), 142–68; Raoul Busquet and Régine Pernoud, *Histoire du commerce de Marseille,* tome I, *Antiquité et moyen âge jusqu'en 1291* (Paris: Librairie Plon, 1949); Hans Van Werveke, *Bruges et Anvers, huit siècles de commerce flammand* (Brussels: Editions de la librairie encyclopédique, 1944); Robert L. Reynolds, "Genoese Trade in the Late Twelfth Century, Particularly in Cloth from the Fairs of Champagne," *Journal of Economic and Business History,* III (1930–31), 362–81; Eleanora M. Carus-Wilson, *Medieval Merchant Venturers* (London: Methuen & Co., Ltd., 1954); and Mollat *et al., op. cit.,* 655–811.

6. The role of Portuguese traders in medieval trade has been recently given its due recognition by Bailey W. Diffie in his *Prelude to Empire. Portugal Overseas before Henry the Navigator* (Lincoln, Nebraska: University of Nebraska Press, 1960).

7. On the wine trade see Margery K. James, "The Fluctuation of the Anglo-Gascon Wine Trade during the Fifteenth Century," *EcHR*, 2d series, IV (1951), 192, Appendix I; and on the wool trade, Eileen Power and M. M. Postan (eds.), *Studies in English Trade in the Fifteenth Century* (London: George Routledge and Sons Ltd., 1933), 39–40.

8. On the brass industry at Dinant see H. Pirenne, "Notice sur l'industrie du laiton à Dinant," and "Les marchands-batteurs de Dinant au xivᵉ et au xvᵉ siècle," *Histoire économique de l'occident médiéval,* ed. E. de Coornaert (Brussels: Desclée de Brouwer & Cie., 1951), 613–20 and 523–31, respectively. An account of the alum trade during the Middle Ages and the Renaissance nicely exemplifying the element of continuity is Leone Laigre's "Le commerce de l'alun en Flandre au moyen âge," *Le moyen âge,* LXI (1955), 177-206.

9. This shipping has been tabulated — see Hughette et Pierre Chaunu, *Seville et l'Atlantique (1504–1650)* (Paris: Librairie Armand Colin, 1955), vols. II and III.

10. For Pera and Genoa see R. S. Lopez in *The Renaissance — A Symposium, February 8–10, 1952* (New York: Metropolitan Museum of Art, 1953), 26, and also in *CEcH*, II, 342; for Marseille, Édouard Baratier and Félix Reynaud, *Histoire du commerce de Marseille*, tome II, *De 1291 à 1480* (Paris: Librairie Plon, 1951), 304–16; for Geneva, Frédéric Borel, *Les foires de Genève au quinzième siècle* (Geneva: H. Georg, Librairie-Editeur, 1892), 272–5; and for Bordeaux, Margery K. James, *op. cit.*, 192–3.

11. Cf. below, 74.

12. The extent and nature of this decline has become a controversial matter. A valuable, recent study, although somewhat disputatious in spirit, is that of R. S. Lopez and H. A. Miskimin, "The Economic Depression of the Renaissance," *EcHR*, 2d series, XIV (1962), 408–26. For a modified appraisal of the decline, at least with respect to Italy, see Gino Luzzatto, *An Economic History of Italy from the Fall of the Roman Empire to the Beginning of the Sixteenth Century*, trans. Philip Jones (London: Routledge and Kegan Paul, 1961), 137–67.

13. R. S. Lopez in the *Symposium*, 26; more exact figures in *CEcH*, II, 339.

14. Robert S. Smith, "Barcelona 'Bills of Mortality' and Population, 1457–1590," *The Journal of Political Economy*, XLIV (1936), 88–89; Abbott Payson Usher, *The Early History of Deposit Banking in Mediterranean Europe*, vol. LXXV of *Harvard Economic Studies* (Cambridge: Harvard University Press, 1943), 345.

15. For Palermo see Usher, *op. cit.*, 345–6; and for Florence, *CEcH*, II, 339.

16. Philippe Wolff, *Commerce et marchands de Toulouse (vers 1350–vers 1450)* (Paris: Librairie Plon, 1954), 73, 68–86; Édouard Baratier, *La démographie provençale du xiiie siècle au xvie siècle, avec chiffres de comparaison pour le xviie siècle, École pratique des hautes études —* VIe section, *Collection démographie et sociétés*, V (Paris: S.E.V.P.E.N., 1961), 75–100, 109–13, 119–24, and all the appendices; Baratier and Reynaud, *op. cit.*, 315.

17. Maurice A. Arnould, *Les dénombrements de foyers dans le comté de Hainaut — xive–xvie siècle* (Brussels: Académie royale de Belgique, 1956), 276–98; especially the graph opposite 278 and the tables on 294–8. This is a superb study on taxation in Hainaut during the Renaissance period.

18. Figures taken from R. S. Smith's review of J. C. Russell's *British Medieval Population* (Albuquerque, New Mexico: University of New Mexico Press, 1948) in *Speculum*, XXIV (1949), 450–2. Russell's figures may be on the low side (J. Krause, "The Medieval Household: Large or Small," *EcHR*, 2d series, IX [1957], 420–32, but this would not alter the relative picture).

19. Eileen Power in *The Cambridge Medieval History*, VII, 723.

20. For eastern Germany see Carsten, *op. cit.*, 106, 111, 113–5, 120, 126, 183, 190–1; for Flanders, H. Pirenne, *Economic and Social History of Medieval Europe*, 173, 195, and Raymond de Roover, *Money, Banking and Credit in Mediaeval Bruges* (Cambridge: The Mediaeval Academy of America, 1948), 250; for Switzerland, *CEcH*, II, 338–9.

21. E. Perroy, "Wage Labour in France in the Later Middle Ages," *EcHR*, 2d series, VIII (1955), 232–9, especially the last two pages.

22. For some evidence showing the effects of the war on France see Émile Lavasseur, *Histoire du commerce de la France* (Paris: Librairie nouvelle de droit et de jurisprudence, 1911–1912), I, 183–4; John Seargeant Cyprian Bridge, *History of France from the Death of Louis XI* (Oxford: Clarendon Press, 1921–1929), I, 20–25; VI, 265–6; and Margery K. James, *op. cit.*, 179ff. and Appendix I, 192.

23. See H. L. Gray's essay, "English Foreign Trade from 1446 to 1482," *Studies in English Trade in the Fifteenth Century*, particularly, 20–24.

24. An excellent account of this trade with the Orient, of its rise in the Middle Ages and of its decline at the beginning of the Renaissance, is R. S. Lopez's "European Merchants in the Medieval Indies: The Evidence of Commercial Documents," *The Journal of Economic History*, III (1943), 164–84. For a brief statement see *CEcH*, II, 339–40.

25. For a suggestive pertinent study see Karl F. Helleiner, "Europas Bevölkerung und Wirtschaft im späteren Mittelalter," *Mitteilungen des Institutes für österreichische Geschichtsforschung*, LXII (1954), 254–69.

26. A partial compilation of the English customs figures is to be found in Eileen Power and M. M. Postan (eds.), *op. cit.*, 330–60, and in Peter Ramsey's "Overseas Trade in the Reign of Henry VII; The Evidence of Customs Accounts," *EcHR*, 2d series, VI (1953), 173–82. The Danish list is to be found in Nina Ellinger Bang, *Tables de la navigation et du transport des marchandises passant le Sund, 1497–1660* (Copenhagen: Cyldendaleke Boghandel, 1906, 1922). Some figures for Antwerp may be found in J. A. Goris, *Étude sur les colonies marchandes méridionales — Portugais, Espagnols, Italiens — a Anvers de 1488 a 1567* (Louvain: Librairies universitaire, 1925). For the rise in Norman commerce see M. Mollat, *Le commerce maritime normand a*

la fin du moyen âge (Paris: Librairie Plon, 1952). For Spain, but dealing only with American trade, see Huguette and Pierre Chaunu, op. cit.

27. For references see G. V. Scammell, "English Merchant Shipping at the End of the Middle Ages: Some East Coast Evidence," EcHR, 2d series, XIII (1961), 339.

28. Exemplified, for instance, by the lot of the lower classes in Hainaut. See H. G. Koenigsberger, "Property and the Price Revolution (Hainaut, 1474–1573)," EcHR, 2d series, IX (1956), 11, 13.

29. One of the most revealing accounts of this prodigal extravagance is to be found in Lawrence Stone's article, "The Anatomy of the Elizabethan Aristocracy," EcHR, XVIII (1948), 3–13. His position has been challenged but not overthrown. There may have been less prodigality but hardly less extravagance. Cf. Gordon R. Batho, "The Finances of an Elizabethan Nobleman: Henry Percy, Ninth Earl of Northumberland (1564–1632)," EcHR, 2d series, IX (1957), 433–50.

30. Quoted from G. G. Coulton, Social Life in Britain from the Conquest to the Reformation (Cambridge: Cambridge University Press, 1919), 380, 385.

31. See Henri Sée, Histoire économique de la France (Paris: Librairie Armand Colin, 1948), I, 61–4, 100–12.

32. The slave trade was considerably more extensive in the Middle Ages than is generally recognized. See Charles Verlinden, L'ésclavage dans l'Europe médiévale, vol. I, Péninsule Ibérique-France (Bruges: De Tempel, 1955).

33. H. V. Livermore, History of Portugal (Cambridge: Cambridge University Press, 1947), 191–2.

34. CEcH, I, 356, n. 1.

35. For his rise see G. G. Coulton, op. cit., 415–20.

36. There are many studies dealing with individual merchants. For two early examples see Margery K. James, "A London Merchant of the Fourteenth Century," EcHR, 2d series, VIII (1956), 364–76; and Robert Brun, "A Fourteenth Century Merchant of Italy: Francesco Datini of Prato," Journal of Economic and Business History, II (1929–30), 451–66. For an example from the late Renaissance period see Henri Lapeyre, Une famille de marchands, les Ruiz (Paris: Librairie Armand Colin, 1955). Although concerned with the famous Spanish merchant family that engaged in French and Spanish commerce, this book actually is a study of the ways of big business in the sixteenth century.

37. E. M. Carus-Wilson, "The English Cloth Industry in the Late Twelfth and Early Thirteenth Centuries," EcHR, XIV (1944–45), 45.

38. On the subject of the fairs see H. Pirenne, *Economic and Social History of Medieval Europe,* 97–103; *CEcH,* III, 126–53; and Mollat *et al., op. cit.,* 746–9.

39. R. S. Lopez, "Majorcans and Genoese on the North Sea Route in the Thirteenth Century," *RB,* XXIX (1951), 1163–79; *CEcH,* III, 133–4.

40. The fairs at Bergen op Zoom afford a classical example of a so-called medieval institution originating in the Renaissance period and lasting throughout it. On these fairs see Nelly J. M. Keerling, "Relations of English Merchants with Bergen op Zoom, 1480–1481," *Bulletin of the Institute of Historical Research,* XXXI (1958), 130–40.

41. See Wolff, *op. cit.,* 454. For other examples and a general treatment of partnerships, see *ibid.,* 483–513 and Lapeyre, *op. cit.,* 143–52.

42. See Frederic Lane's interesting study "Family Partnerships and Joint Ventures in the Venetian Republic," *The Journal of Economic History,* IV (1944), 178–96.

43. See Raymond de Roover, "The Story of the Alberti Company of Florence, 1302–1348, as Revealed in Its Account Books," *The Business History Review,* XXXII (1958), 14–60.

44. On this type of partnership see *CEcH,* III, 107.

45. Gordon Connell-Smith, *Forerunners of Drake* ("Royal Empire Society Imperial Studies"; London: Longmans, Green and Co., 1954), 81–99.

46. An excellent account of the evolution of the company is provided by E. M. Carus-Wilson in her *Medieval Merchant Venturers,* 143–82. The regulations of the company may be found in W. E. Lingelbach, *The Merchant Adventurers of England: their Laws and Ordinances* ("University of Pennsylvania, Translations and Reprints," 2d series, II, Philadelphia).

47. On these two examples of "mixed" organizations see Heers, *Gênes au xvᵉ siècle,* 385–7, 202–3, respectively.

48. For a recent treatment of the decline, which introduces several new considerations, see John Allyne Gade, *The Hanseatic Control of Norwegian Commerce during the Late Middle Ages* (Leiden: E. J. Brill, 1951).

49. An up-to-date study on the bill of exchange is Raymond de Roover's *L'évolution de la lettre de change, xivᵉ–xviiiᵉ siècle* (Paris: Librairie Armand Colin, 1953).

50. On the relation between the bill of exchange and the notarial contract, see *ibid.,* 25–42, and Wolff, *op. cit.,* 384–6.

51. *Ibid.,* 385; also R. de Roover, *L'évolution de la lettre de change, xivᵉ–xviiiᵉ siècle,* 38–39.

52. An excellent survey of the history of insurance with a number of examples is Florence Edler de Roover's "Early Examples of Marine Insurance," *The Journal of Economic History,* V (1945), 172–201.

53. *Ibid.,* 186–7.

54. *Ibid.,* 183.

55. For actual documents covering this and other examples, see R. S. Lopez and Irving W. Raymond, *Medieval Trade in the Mediterranean World,* no. 52 of *Records of Civilization, Sources and Studies,* ed. Austin P. Evans (New York: Columbia University Press, 1955), 256–65. For additional examples see Florence Edler de Roover, *op. cit.,* 190–6.

56. Jacques Heers, *Le livre de comptes de Giovanni Piccamiglio, Homme d'affaires Génois, 1456–1459, École pratique des hautes études* — VIᵉ section. *Centre de recherches historiques, Affaires et gens d'affaires,* XII (Paris: S.E.V.P.E.N., 1959), 31.

57. For the individual entries in Cambi's books see the tables in Florence Edler de Roover, *op. cit.,* 192–3.

58. Edward Paragallo, *Origin and Evolution of Double Entry Bookkeeping* (New York: American Institute Publishing Co., 1938), 3, 27.

59. *Ibid.,* 55–60.

60. Mildred L. Hartsough, "A New Treatise on Bookkeeping under the Fuggers," *Journal of Economic and Business History,* IV (1932), 539–51.

61. Raymond de Roover," "The Story of the Alberti Company of Florence, 1302–1348, as Revealed in Its Account Books," *The Business History Review,* XXXII (1958), 33–34.

62. Dorothea D. Reeves, "Sixteenth-Century Writings on Bookkeeping Acquired by the Kress Library of Business and Economics," *The Business History Review,* XXIV (1960), 327–34.

III

Power, New Machines, and New Industries

Wind and Water Power The Renaissance period began with one revolution in industry practically completed, namely, the utilization of two natural forces for power purposes; for it was in the Middle Ages, especially from the eleventh century on, that wind and water were harnessed to work for man. All over Europe, windmills and water wheels by the thousands were employed to power all sorts of mills — flour, paper, fulling, tanning, and wood-turning mills — and various machines in the mining and metallurgical industries — ore crushers, bellows, forge-hammers, and chain-and-bucket water pumps. And how extensive this revolution was can be surmised from the fact that in England, even as early as the Domesday survey (1086), there were no less than 5,624 water mills south of the rivers Trent and Severn.[1] On the other hand, no new source of power was discovered during the Renaissance period — in fact, the world had to wait for the steam engine before another revolution of equal proportions would materialize — so that in respect to this very important aspect of industry the Renaissance saw continuity rather than a revolution.

Changes in Machinery Not quite so lacking in change were the machines that were used during the Renaissance; for, while most of the machinery of the period was inherited from antiquity and the Middle Ages, some machines underwent considerable improvement or were applied in new ways, and some new ones were invented.

In the cloth industry, especially in the making of silk, silk-throwing mills were developed with multiple rows of spindles and reels, some capable of driving as many as 480 spindles. Developed in Lucca by the end of the Middle Ages, the invention was carried to Florence and Venice about the middle of the fourteenth century, that is, at the beginning of the Renaissance period. The machine cut the number of workers, "throwers," from several hundred to two or three operators, thereby promising to revolutionize one phase of the silk industry.[2] However, there is no indication that the invention spread widely throughout Europe before 1550.

In the metallurgical industries, the high blast furnace with water-driven bellows appeared in the first half of the fourteenth century. Its bellows provided a constant instead of an intermittent blast of air and generated enough heat to liquify the iron, so that it was capable of producing two or three times as much iron per year — 40 to 50 tons — as could be processed by the simpler forges known as the "bloomeries." But it, too, did not expand rapidly during the Renaissance. It did not reach northern Italy until 1450, and its penetration into France, and then only into limited areas, did not come until about the end of the fifteenth century; while there were only three such furnaces in England at the beginning of the sixteenth century and only six or seven as late as 1539. For its widespread adoption, Europe had to wait until the century 1540–1640.[3] In mining, the rag and chain pump and the reversible wheel used to operate it appeared toward the end of the fifteenth century, but their high cost limited their adoption until the second half of the sixteenth century when greater amounts of capital became available.

Of general applicability were the crank and the connecting rod which if combined could give a continuous rotary motion. The crank, of course, was an ancient invention, but its combination with a connecting rod did not appear until early in the fifteenth century. The combination, however, failed to gain widespread adoption. Appearing more frequently from the fifteenth century on were boring machines for hollowing out wheel drums, logs for wooden pipes, and for reaming out bores of cannon.[4]

Not a machine in a literal sense of the term, unless we regard it as a transportation engine, was the three-masted ship which was developed in the Renaissance period. The hull was of the caravel variety, that is, a modified form of the medieval round cargo carrier, but the important innovation was the adoption of three masts to make sailing possible in wind from almost any direction. It was this kind of vessel which made ocean voyages possible. The first dated picture of such a ship comes from the year 1466, but the ship undoubtedly must have appeared earlier.

NEW INDUSTRIES Of greater impact on Renaissance economy than the change in machinery, was the introduction of new industries, new in the full sense of the term, and new in the sense of greater geographical expansion.

Completely new industries were printing and the manufacturing of cannons and light firearms and the necessary supplies of saltpeter and gunpowder. The making of alum from alunite deposits discovered in Tolfa, Italy, about 1450 may also be included among the new industries in Europe proper. For obvious reasons all these industries grew rapidly, but mostly in the last century of the Renaissance. It is estimated, for example, that Lyon, the principal printing center in France, had upwards of 150 printers by 1550 and that European presses produced close to 12,000,000 books by the same date and perhaps twice as many again in the next fifty years.[5]

Belonging to the other category of new industries were paper making, silkmaking, glassmaking, brassmaking, and wire drawing. All were known in the Middle Ages, but it was in the Renaissance period, especially after the middle of the fifteenth century when the standard of living rose, that these industries expanded throughout Europe. Silkmaking in France may be taken as an example of the phenomenal rise. To expand this industry in his kingdom Louis XI brought some silkmakers to Lyon in 1466. Four years later, because of opposition from the townsmen, he transferred the industry to Tours. According to reports only sixteen craftsmen started the operation at the new location, yet by the year 1500 there were some 800 master craftsmen and 4,000 workers, and by 1550 the number involved had doubled. The success of the industry at Tours led to its re-introduction in Lyon in 1536, where by 1550 it employed some 5,000 workers, and to its spread to Nîmes, Montpellier, and Paris.[6] Although its expansion elsewhere in northern Europe was less phenomenal, still its growth in France is quite suggestive of the significance that geographical expansion of an old industry might have.

Surveying these three aspects of industry, we can point to the invention of some new machines and to the introduction of some new industries, but to no change in the source of power. We could not therefore expect any major transformation of industry during the Renaissance, even if we see signs of substantial changes to come thereafter.

However, before we draw any firm conclusions, we need to ascertain whether there were any changes in the ways industry was organized and in the volume of its output.

Forms of Industry

USUFACTURE During the Renaissance, as in the Middle Ages, the primary form of industry was household industry or usufacture as it is sometimes called. Most of the peasants and many of the townsmen fashioned with their own hands much of what they needed for themselves, their homes, and their farms. Specialization and modern sophistication had not yet reached the point where men could not use the craftsman's tools and ladies used the spinning wheel for decoration only. Their skills, if not professional, were sufficient for their simple needs, and their hands and fingers were strong and nimble.

CRAFT SHOP AND GILD[7] The second type of industry which prevailed during the Renaissance, as well as in the preceding era, was the small shop with a craftsman master as head and operator and one or more apprentices as learners and assistants. There the raw materials were fashioned into finished or semifinished articles, and there some of them were sold. As in the Middle Ages, craftsmen belonging to the same trade were organized locally in craft gilds, whose elected officers drew up regulations governing such matters as prices, standards of workmanship, conditions for admission to the gild, length and terms of apprenticeship, and requirements for admission to mastership.

Although prevalent throughout the entire Renaissance period, the gild system did not remain rigid but responded more or less readily to certain economic developments of the day.

One of the responses was the tendency toward exclusivism. The trend had begun in the Middle Ages, but it became strong in the first century of the Renaissance, when the depression described in the preceding chapter prompted the gilds to adopt certain protective measures which made them more exclusive and monopolistic. In general, the gilds tightened their admission and advancement policies to prevent oversaturation of their respective trades, and they did so by raising the entry fees, by banning admission of "foreigners," that is, of migrant craftsmen from other towns, by lengthening the apprenticeship period, by demanding more exacting masterpieces, and by requiring the candidate to have sufficient capital to set himself up in business.[8] On the other hand, they tried to make the membership hereditary; and apparently with great success if Gand is any example, for in that city the butchers' and the fishmongers' gilds were actually closed to outsiders by 1325, the bargemen's gild by 1400, and in other gilds, in each thirty-year period from 1420 to 1539, the percentage of outsiders admitted into the gilds dropped from about 24 per cent to 5.7 per cent to 4.3 per cent to zero.[9] At the same time there was considerable intermarriage among the principal members, which contributed to this exclusivism still more. Then, to secure their position in the public, the gilds secured charters from the crown, engaged actively in municipal politics, and played up their religious and civic functions, providing emergency relief to their brethren and participating in common and in distinctive liveries in the various church and town festivals.[10] The result of all this was the hardening of the gilds into more or less closed corporations with all the attendant practices of restriction and monopoly that go with such corporations.

Of course, this trend was not universal, nor was its pace uniform. Indeed, there were towns where the depressed economic situations sometimes necessitated the reversal of the trend, that is, the dissolution of the gilds and the restoration of "free" industry. At Chartres, for example, in 1416, the royal bailiff proclaimed the liberty of commerce and industry because of the misery of the town. But such reversals were the exception rather than the rule. Besides, they did not affect the craft shop system of organization, which remained unchanged.

This hardening of gilds necessarily led to certain countertrends. One was the "flight" of some industries or phases thereof to the countryside where the gild restrictions were inoperative. To be sure, the shift from manual to water power was a contributing factor in many instances, and in some industries it was undoubtedly the principal reason; but the fact that some industries which did not use water power also moved outside the towns is strong proof that many transfers must have been prompted by the desire to escape the monopolistic policies of the gilds and the higher costs of production which this monopoly engendered. Another consequence of this hardening was the rise of journeymen unions and the resultant friction between them and the regular gilds. Because of the restrictive policies of the masters, many journeymen found it difficult to attain the master's status and so had to remain as journeymen. The poor economic conditions of the period aggravated their distress, as industry could not readily absorb the yearly crop of journeymen many of whom were therefore forced to take to the road in search of employment. Their plight prompted them to organize themselves into unions in the hope of improving their "bargaining" position in relation to the masters and, indeed, in relation to society in general. The movement was suspect, and in some Italian towns was actually banned; but in England, Germany, and France it reached substantial proportions, especially in France where the badly depressed state of economy until about 1450 simply made such unions inevitable.

In the second century of the Renaissance and directly connected with the economic recovery of the period, two trends appeared which actually fostered the gilds.

One of these was simply the multiplication of gilds necessitated by the revival of industry. In many instances, extension of industries to new localities led to the organization of the craftsmen involved into appropriate gilds in these localities. In other cases, the population increase and the economic upswing led to the restoration of old gilds and the creation of new ones. In Poitiers, for example, a dozen new gilds came into being in the last half of the fifteenth century. In Rome, too, whereas there were only eighteen gilds by the year 1400, fourteen new ones appeared in the fifteenth century, and twenty-three more in the sixteenth century. Thus also in sixteenth-century Exeter, where, according to a recent study, "the traditional structure of economic life was not only preserved but positively strengthened," at least six new gilds appeared between 1561 and 1586.[11]

Another trend, both multiplying and solidifying the gilds, was the increase in state intervention. The rising New Monarchies were interested in enlarging the resources of their states and in improving the general welfare of their people, and both of these required the stimulation of national economies. In general, this took the form of promoting expansion of industry by authorizing appropriate artisans to initiate the industry and by giving them certain privileges, including the right to

form a gild — indeed, in most cases they were encouraged or even required to organize themselves into a gild. Louis XI, for example, eager
to see the industry in Tours revived, ordered in 1481 all the crafts in the
city to organize themselves into gilds. Often, also, this promotion took
the form of the nationalization of some gild regulations. In the Middle
Ages, gild regulations were local, each gild in each town having its own
rules. While this served the interests of the local gilds, it naturally handi-
capped economic planning for the nation as a whole and had to be
eliminated or at least curtailed. Sometimes the gilds took the initiative
themselves, out of self-interest, by confederating and compiling uniform
rules for a wide region, as in the case of the builders' gilds of Strasbourg,
Cologne, Vienna, and Zurich which federated in 1454 and agreed on
a common body of regulations. But it was the state for the most part
that pushed this program forward. In France, for example, Louis XI's
ordinance of 1479 extended the regulations of the Paris gild of woolen
clothmakers to their counterparts throughout his domain, and subsequently additional laws covering other crafts were enacted to the same
end. In Gand, Charles V reduced the number of gilds, requiring the consolidation of some gilds with others, deprived them of the right to elect
their own heads, reduced the entry fees, and opened the gilds to outsiders by voiding the rule that membership was only to be open to sons
of masters. Even if these measures were not fully implemented, they
are nevertheless illustrative of increasing royal interference. In England,
Elizabeth's Statute of Artificers of 1563 combined some of the old restrictive rules with new anti-restrictive ones and made them national
in scope, and all for the sake of the country's economic betterment.

Thus throughout the Renaissance, whether the economy was falling
or rising, the gild system and the craft shop remained the mainstay of
industrial organization. The facts that some gilds disintegrated and
that journeymen's unions came into existence should not be taken as
signs of the demise of either the gilds or the craft shop. The day of their
eclipse was still far off.

PUTTING-OUT SYSTEM The third type of industrial organization was
the putting-out system. The system was adopted in several different
industries but it was most widely used in the manufacture of textiles. A
trader in cloth purchased the raw wool and distributed it, personally or

through factors, among the different artisans who prepared it for spinning, and then among numerous housewives in the area who converted it into yarn. This was then paid for at piece-rates, picked up, and distributed among the weavers who wove the yarn into cloth. Sometimes, in addition to the raw product, necessary instruments of production were also supplied. The woven cloth was then collected and paid for on a piece-rate basis, and more raw material was left for fabrication. After this process in manufacture, the dealers contracted with the fullers, dyers, and various other finishers to have definite quantities of cloth fulled, dyed, and finished at agreed prices. When the cloth was ready for the sales counter, the dealer sold it, made his profit, and then repeated the whole series of operations. Since the dealer never lost ownership of the material from the first processing stage until it was sold as a finished product, and since he provided all the capital that was needed to buy the raw product, to pay the various fabricators, and to market the finished goods, and since some of the wealthier entrepreneurs had their own shops where some of the fabricating processes were carried out by paid labor, this type of industry is usually distinguished from the gild-form and is often regarded as capitalistic.

Although this type of industry was admittedly capitalistic, it was not a vast industry organized in factories and owned and operated by a few industrial tycoons. The entrepreneurs who were engaged in the textile industry were relatively numerous — in Milan, for example, there were 363 firms in the late fourteenth century — generally only of moderate wealth, and often organized in small partnerships with correspondingly small capitalization. Their establishments were obviously not factories, but small shops which were operated in accordance with gild principles, and which certainly were not equipped to carry out all the processing steps. Finally, the whole industry was still partially gild-organized: the entrepreneurs, in the gilds of cloth dealers; and some of the fabricators, in the different artisan gilds. Thus the industry, while admitting some capitalistic features, was still close to the medieval gild system.

FACTORY-TYPE INDUSTRY Still another form of industry was the factory system. This system required not only concentration of capital, but also concentration of labor and a plant. In the Middle Ages, if we exclude small establishments like the water-driven fulling and paper mills, many of which employed two or more workmen and so may well be regarded as miniature factories, and some wire-pulling shops like those established in Frankfurt, Augsburg, and Nuremberg,[12] or such large establishments as Benedetto Zaccaria's alum works in Phocaea and the state rope factory, the Tana, which was established in Venice in 1303,[13] this type of industrial organization was practically unknown. In the Renaissance, it was beginning to make its appearance and was therefore still rudimentary in organization, small in scale, and affected only a few industries.

In connection with the cloth industry two developments were promoting the factory system. In the dyeing process large vats were making their appearance. These required more money than one dyer could raise, and so several men pooled their capital, erected a large vat, and employed a few additional workers to help them dye the cloth. The resulting establishment was a rudimentary factory. Considerably larger than these dyeing establishments was the plant at Tolfa, Italy, for the processing of alum, a mineral used for dyeing. It was opened in 1461 and within ten years its production mounted to upwards of 3,000 tons annually. Larger than either of the foregoing, if it were possible to believe the English poet Thomas Deloney (1543–1600), was the cloth factory of John Winchcombe of Westbury, England. The poet would have the reader believe that:

> Within one room being large and long
> There stood two hundred looms full strong.
> Two hundred men the truth is so
> Wrought in these looms all in a row.
> By every one a pretty boy
> Sate making quills with mickle joy.
> And in another place hard by
> An hundred women merrily
> Were carding hard with joyful cheer
> Who singing sate with voices clear.
> And in a chamber close beside,
> Two hundred maidens did abide
> In petticoats of Stammell red,
> And milk-white kerchers on their head.[14]

Two hundred men, 200 "pretty boys," 100 women, and 200 maidens — 700 laborers in one factory of the famous John Winchcombe! But these

are the figures of a poet born about twenty-three years after the death of Winchcombe (d.1520), and who was only twenty-two years old when the son and successor of John was no more. At the most the poet's picture can be accepted only as evidence of a substantial cloth factory; while his interest in the plant at all can be taken as an indication of the recentness of the factory. It might be safe therefore to say that cloth factories employing 100 to 200 workers appeared in the sixteenth century.

This appearance of textile mills in sixteenth-century England should not be regarded as a sign of any widespread adoption of them on the continent. Indeed, there is some reason to believe that the very idea of concentrating men and machines in one large building could not take root in the minds of the European clothiers of that time. An excellent illustration of this fact comes from Poitiers where the city fathers and the drapers failed to establish a factory when they could have done so at the time when the French monarchy lent its support to a reorganization of the industry in that city. In 1488 the city council received from Charles VIII a subvention of 1,000 *livres* and exemption from impost on all raw materials needed for the manufacture of cloth and on the finished cloth itself. On January 23, 1489, the council ordered all the merchant drapers to bring their "presses" to the city hall to be purchased by the municipality, apparently with the view "of assembling all the equipment in just a single place in order to establish at Poitiers a great textile industry." In 1501, instead of a factory there was merely an association of merchant drapers under the supervision of the council, each operating independently and employing his own workers.[15] The old system of industrial organization was simply too hard to displace, and even after eighty years of operation, until 1589 when the association was dissolved, it remained unchanged. Apparently, neither the city officials nor the merchants could conceive of a new way of organizing the industry.

MINING AS A FACTORY-TYPE INDUSTRY It is customary to regard the factory system as being more advanced in the mining and metallurgical industries than in the cloth industry. This view appears to be correct and is confirmed by facts. The salt mines at Halle, Wielcszka, and Salins were worked on a large scale; the processing plant at Salins, for

example, Grande Saunerie as it was called, occupied an area 300 yards
by 100 yards. Iron, silver, copper, and coal-mining industries expanded
likewise to meet the demands of the growing armaments industry and
the increasing needs for bullion. New deposits were located and old
mines were reopened and both were worked to a greater depth, requiring more men, equipment, and money, and evolving into sizable establishments physically and financially. Increased depth necessitated larger
and more efficient pumping and ventilating machines, some driven by
water wheels, and these were costly and required several operators.
High-blast furnaces, as indicated above, began to replace the less costly
smelting forges called "bloomeries," and the increased size of the
"blooms" (pasty iron mass) which these furnaces produced necessitated
replacement of the manually operated hammers by much heavier hammers driven by water power. A new process for extracting silver from
argentiferous copper ore, with copper as a joint product, was discovered
about 1451 and led to a more thorough exploitation of the copper deposits. Joint-stock companies, like the Society of Mines Royal and the
Society of the Mineral and Battery Works in England, or like the Genoese Society, Mahona de l'ile d'Elbe, which controlled the iron mined in
Elba, were being organized to meet the high financial demands entailed
by all this progress.[16]

This trend toward a capitalistic and factory-type organization in the
mining industry, however, was only a trend as yet in the Renaissance.
For one thing, some of the changes enumerated above were slow to
expand widely. The high-blast furnace, it will be recalled, spread very
slowly and did not gain universal acceptance until after the Renaissance
period. The same applies to the improved pump, the rag and chain
pump, and the reversible water wheel used to operate the pump, which
came into wide use only after the middle of the sixteenth century. Until
that time, of course, the bucket and the windlass, operated manually,
did the task.[17] For another thing, there were certain problems which
defied solution for the time being and so precluded expansion which
might have led to large establishments needing sizable amounts af capital. Ventilation for example was one of these; and without ventilation
there was a limit to expansion possibilities. Miners had to avoid sinking deep shafts and had to be content with shafts that averaged twenty

to thirty feet, although shafts of eighty feet and more were not uncommon. Another was the method of breaking off pieces of rock from the ore vein. The pick, the wedge, and the shovel can only do so much. Hence until the advent of blasting about 1610 — it did not reach England until 1670 — expansion could not be great.[18] In general therefore, in view of these retardations and limitations, the mining and metallurgical industries were slow in assuming the factory-type organization.[19]

Turning from the mechanics to the organization of mining enterprises, we will find a similar tardiness. There were four prevailing types of mining organization. One was the association of co-workers whose members secured the right to work a mine and who labored with their own hands. Another was the cost system, which was similar to the partnership with the exception that members were permitted to commute their labor obligations for regular money payments or to engage substitute laborers. The tribute system was the third type; it permitted the association to assign a portion of its claim to outside individuals to work it as they saw fit in return for a share ranging from one-half to one-seventh of the yield. And the fourth was the lease system, which permitted an outside party to lease part of the works of an association. All four of these types persisted from the Middle Ages and underwent little change during the Renaissance. They tended to become more and more capitalistic, but the tendency had begun before the Renaissance. Indeed, these variations in organization were themselves nothing else but ways and means of raising more capital for the operations. Ownership of mine shares by churchmen, merchants, nobles, and women, that is, by persons who were not likely to labor in the industry, appear in the records early and certainly show the penetration of capital into the mining industry. The famous alum mine of Benedetto Zaccaria, though dating back to the thirteenth century, was definitely capitalistic. The leasing of some royal mines by Edward I of England to the Frescobaldi house of Florence in 1299, and the operations of one "Abraham the Tinner," who in 1357 is reported to have owned two mine works and four stream works in which he employed over 300 men, women, and children, show very clearly that by the time of the Renaissance the mining industry had already admitted capitalistic ways, and that in some

instances it also partook of the factory system.[20] What happened to this
trend during the Renaissance was an increase in its tempo and a gradual
displacement of simple partnerships by joint-stock companies. But the
first development came after 1450 and the second even later, so that
real acceleration was belated — not until the end of the Renaissance.

STATE PLANTS The largest single plants in operation in Europe during the Renaissance times were the arsenals. The arsenal at Venice, in
1540, occupied sixty acres of space, employed between 1,000 and 2,000
workmen, used the belt system of construction, and could complete a
ship from keel to mast in a short time and "de-moth" one in a few
hours. But this plant was operated as a state enterprise and not as a
private business. Furthermore, it was of medieval origin and, as Professor Nef points out, it was already so vast and bustling in the time of
Dante that the poet used it to draw his picture of the Fifth Chasm in
the Inferno.[21] Another large arsenal was "l'Artillerie" at Nancy, a
property owned by the dukes of Lorraine. By 1503 it was already of considerable importance, including furnaces, forges, cannon foundries,
gunpowder mills, saltpeter shops, even corn mills for grinding flour
for the workers in the arsenal, and occupying several acres of ground.[22]
Somewhat smaller arsenals were being operated in Sussex and Kent in
England.

SUMMARY In summary, the organization of industry during the
Renaissance underwent some changes, but these did not amount to a
revolution. Usufacture continued without change, except that it de-
creased as more people bought finished goods than in the Middle Ages.
The gild system persisted, but it came more and more under national
control and began also to yield to engrossment and to the invasion of
capitalism. The putting-out system, also a carry-over from the Middle
Ages,[23] began to expand with the greater penetration of capitalism.
Only the factory system was relatively new. Potentially, because it was
capable of harnessing large amounts of capital, it promised a great transformation of European industry, and indeed it began to take effect about
1550,[24] but in the Renaissance this form was still small and crude and
at times even beyond the ken of those in position to implement it.
Hence its impact was not great.

Volume of Industrial Output

The slowness in the adoption of factories naturally precluded any phenomenal rise in industrial output. Nevertheless, there was some increase, as other factors contributed to the growth of industry. The upturn in population and in the resulting consumer demand in the second half of the Renaissance period led to some advance. The rising standard of living among the bourgeoisie and the patriciate stimulated increased production of fine apparel and expensive furnishings. New industries, new in the full sense of the word — such as those of saltpeter and gunpowder making, cannon casting, brassmaking, and printing — or new in the sense only of becoming significantly more widespread than they were before — such as brickmaking, silkmaking, and sugar refining — added their output to the volume. England's transformation in the fourteenth and fifteenth centuries, from a wool-producing to a cloth-manufacturing nation, multiplied the output of its looms eightfold. Expanding oceanic navigation called for more shipbuilding. State demands for precious metals and armaments and the depletion of forests necessitated an increase in coal and metal mining and in metallurgical industries. There are indications, for example, that "the output of iron and copper in central Europe increased rapidly during the last half of the fifteenth century and the early decades of the sixteenth"; that "Styria, perhaps the greatest iron-making center, was turning out four times as much iron in 1536 as in 1466"; that "in Germany, Hungary, and the Eastern Alps, the production of copper probably increased even more rapidly than that of iron," and that of silver "perhaps more than fivefiold."[25] Thus also, production of coal in England increased comparably: whereas before the sixteenth century approximately 15,000 tons were shipped annually from the fields on the lower Tyne, whence came about three-fourths of the nation's coal at the time, the shipments rose to about 32,000 tons in the decade from 1541 to 1550 and to about 50,000 tons some twenty years later.[26] Hence the total volume of industrial production was undoubtedly considerably greater than in the preceding age.

But the increase, while substantial, was not of such proportions as to transform Renaissance society from an agrarian to an industrial one. The increased standard of living was met only partially by native industry, for some of the luxury goods, such as rich cloth, silk, tapestries and rugs, and gold ornaments, were still imported from the Near or the Far East. If there were more grand residences and civic buildings erected during the Renaissance than during the Middle Ages, there was a corresponding decrease in the building of castles and monasteries, for the period of robust feudalism and extensive castle building was coming to a close,[27] and the age of a thriving and an expanding monasticism and therefore of monastery building was over. Indeed, it is quite possible that the drop in population and the cessation of expansion of many of the continental medieval towns after the middle of the fourteenth century brought about some decline in the entire building industry. The increase in shipbuilding activities in Portugal, Spain, England, and the Netherlands to meet the growing oceanic traffic and the expansion of state navies were partially offset by the decline of shipbuilding in Venice during the second half of the fifteenth century — probably because of the gradual depletion of oak forests in its domain[28] — and presumably in other Italian ports also. Similarly the increase in the output of English woolens and Spanish silks was offset by a substantial drop in the production in Flanders and Tuscany. It would seem that the only industries in which the increase was not partially offset were the new industries and the mining and metallurgical industries. But even in some of these industries everything was not net gain. In the armaments industry, for example, the manufacture of cannon and of lead and iron shot was naturally counterbalanced by the drop in the construction of the medieval engines of war — such as ballistae and mangonels — and in quarrying and fashioning of stone balls for them. Thus, where an English sheriff of 1333 would contract with thirty-seven masons to fashion 606 stone balls,[29] the royal official of the sixteenth century would employ a certain number of iron-forgers to cast an equal number of iron balls. The change from medieval batteries to Renaissance artillery was therefore not a complete gain for industrialization. Thus also the gain in industrialization represented by the introduction of light firearms was offset by the loss in the manufacture of shields, rapidly becoming obsolete. Charles of Anjou, for example, once ordered from the Pisan leather workers "upwards of 4,000 shields."[30] No such orders would be forthcoming in the era of the arquebus, and so the manufacture of firearms did not constitute a clear gain for industrialization. Similarly, when the discovery of calamine in England in 1566 led to brassmaking, the resulting manufacture of brass utensils cut into the pewter market and brought about a sizable drop in tin mining.[31] Furthermore, some of the new industries, as the manufacture of saltpeter and paper, were conducted in part as household industries and so did not contribute much to the industrialization of society; while still others, like silkmaking, were slow in rooting themselves north of the Alps and with one or two exceptions, as in the case of the silk industry of Tours, were not really significant before the seventeenth century. Even mining and metallurgical industries, the very industries that increased manifold, did not employ a great number of people and did not have a very extensive output. Charles V's estimate that there were hundreds of thousands of workers in these industries in Germany is certainly an exaggerated estimate, for the entire Shwaz region, probably the most heavily mined area in the country, had only some 20,000 workers, and the biggest mining and smelting combine in the land, the Fugger-Thurzo firm, which had a near monopoly on Hungarian, Tyrolese, and on much of German copper-mining industry, employed only "several hundred workers."[32] Even less impressive are the figures regarding the output of iron in England. If we accept Professor Nef's estimate that the output of iron in England increased about fivefold between 1540 and 1640 and that on the eve of the Civil War England produced a minimum of 20,000 tons and a maximum of 43,000 tons,[33] we will see that the output about 1540, that is, at the height of the Renaissance, ranged between 4,000 and 8,000 tons. This is not an output that suggests a large-scale industry. Hence, taking all things into account, we must conclude that the net increase in industry during the Renaissance, while admittedly substantial, was not of revolutionary proportions.

In three aspects of industry we noticed some changes. Some completely new industries made their appearance and some that were known in the Middle Ages but were confined to the Mediterranean lands were extended throughout much of northern Europe. In organization the putting-out system grew in use and the factory made its appearance. But while both had disintegrating effects on the basic organization (the gild), the gilds persisted throughout the Renaissance, hardened by the century of depression and subjected ever more thoroughly by the rising states. In volume, largely because of improved standards of living, because of some new industries, and because of greater need for metals, especially for armaments, there was a noticeable increase. But in the one aspect which would be likely to have the greatest impact, namely in the use of power, there was no change whatsoever. Hence our conclusion would have to be that there was no substantial transformation of industry during the Renaissance period.

1. On the great increase in the number and use of wind and water mills, see Charles Singer *et al.* (eds.), *A History of Technology* (Oxford: Clarendon Press, 1956), II, 609–10.

2. *Ibid.,* II, 206–7.

3. On the spread of the high-blast furnace see Ernest Straker, *Wealden Iron* (London: G. Bell and Sons, Ltd., 1931), 38–59. For a detailed account of its development and spread in England, see H. R. Schubert, *History of the British Iron and Steel Industry from c. 450 B.C. to A.D. 1775* (London: Routledge and Kegan Paul, 1957), chapters ix–xii and Appendix V. For Genoa see Heers, *Gênes au xvᵉ siècle,* 219–23. Cf. also J. U. Nef, "A Comparison of Industrial Growth in France and England from 1540 to 1640, II," *The Journal of Political Economy,* XLIV (1936), 516–7.

4. Singer *et al., op. cit.,* II, 651–4.

5. On the expansion of printing see my *The Renaissance,* III, *Education, Learning, and Thought* (Salt Lake City: University of Utah Press, 1963), 189–92.

6. Myron P. Gilmore, *The World of Humanism, 1453–1517* (New York: Harper & Brothers Publishers, 1952), 53, and Henri Sée, *Histoire économique de la France* (Paris: Librairie Armand Colin, 1948), I, 121.

7. Much information on this subject is available in *CEcH,* III, chaps. iv and v, *passim.*

8. For some examples of exclusivism on the continent as well as in England see L. Brentano's essay on the gilds in Toulmin Smith *et al., English Gilds,* no. 40 of *Early English Text Society,* original series, (1870), cxix–cxx, cxlviii–cli.

9. On the exclusivism in Gand see Hans Van Werveke, *Gand, esquisse d'histoire sociale* (Paris: La Renaissance du Livre, 1946), 53–55.

10. For details on the structure and functions of these confraternities see the numerous charters in Toulmin Smith *et al., op. cit.,* parts I and II.

11. On these increases see Jean Delumeau, *Vie économique et sociale de Rome dans la seconde moitié du xvi siècle,* no. 184 of *Bibliothèque des écoles françaises d'Athènes et de Rome* (Paris, 1957), I, 368–9; Wallace T. MacCaffrey, *Exeter, 1540–1640, The Growth of an English County Town* (Cambridge: Harvard University Press, 1958), 87–89.

12. On the establishment of wire-pulling shops see Eric E. Hirshler, "Medieval Economic Competition," *The Journal of Economic History,* XIV (1954), 55–57, and the references cited therein.

13. On these two large establishments see *CEcH,* II, 336–7, and C. Lane, "The Rope Factory and Hemp Trade of Venice in the Fifteenth and Sixteenth Centuries," *Journal of Economic and Business History,* IV (1931–32), 830–47.

14. Quoted from *The Works of Thomas Deloney,* ed. F. O. Mann (Oxford: Clarendon Press, 1912), 20–21.

15. On this episode see P. Boissonnade, *Essai sur l'organization du travail en Poitou depuis le xie siècle jusqu'a la revolution* (Paris: H. Champion, 1900), II, 391–6. Cf. also P. Raveau, *Essai sur la situation économique et l'état social en Poitou au xvie siècle* (Paris: Librairie des sciences politiques et sociales, 1931), 5–10.

16. For a fuller treatment of some of these advances consult *CEcH,* II, 458–80, and Singer *et al., op. cit.,* II, 13–24. For England, the best account is to be found in Schubert, *op. cit.,* chaps. ix–xii. For Genoa see Heers, *Gênes au xve siècle,* 219–23.

17. Cf., for example, the operations in the coal mine of Earl of Shrewsbury as related in Lawrence Stone, "An Elizabethan Coal Mine," *EcHR,* 2d series, III (1950), 98.

18. George Randall Lewis, *The Stannaries, A Study of the English Tin Miner,* vol. III of *Harvard Economic Studies* (Cambridge: 1924), 12–14, 23.

19. Cf. Nef in *CEcH,* II, 460.

20. For a brief résumé of mining techniques and organization in the Middle Ages and in the Renaissance see Lewis, *op. cit.,* 177–83, 185–92; *CEcH,* II, 458–69; Leon Schick, *Un grand homme d'affaires au début du xvie siècle — Jacob Fugger, École pratique des hautes études — VIe section, Centre de recherches historiques, Affaires et gens d'affaires,* XI (Paris: S. E. V. P. E. N., 1957), 254–75.

21. *The Divine Comedy,* trans. J. B. Fletcher (New York: Macmillan Co., 1933), Inferno, Canto xxi, 7–15.

22. Nef, "War and Economic Progress," *EcHR,* XII (1942), 22–23.

23. For evidence see above, 36; *CEcH,* II, 381–98; Georges Espinas, *Les origines du capitalisme. I. Sire Jehan Boinebroke, Patricien et drapier dousiaien, ?–1236 environ* (Lille: Librairie E. Raoust, 1933).

24. Professor Nef, in all his writings on this subject, seems to be so enthusiastic about the extent of this industrial growth in the century 1540–1640 that he considers it as a prototype of the Industrial Revolution.

25. Nef, "War and Economic Progress, 1540–1640," *EcHR,* XII (1942), 26; *CEcH,* II, 470.

26. J. U. Nef, *The Rise of the British Coal Industry* (London: George Routledge & Sons, Ltd., 1932), I, 9–10, 11, 360, and the chart opposite 380.

27. Note the drop in England from 181 castles in the reign of Edward III, to sixty in the reign of his son, to eight in the reign of Henry IV, to one under Henry V, five in the time of Henry VI, and three in the time of Edward IV (H. D. Traill and J. C. Mann, eds., *Social England* [New York: G. P. Putnam's Sons, 1902], II, 494).

28. Frederic C. Lane, "Venetian Shipping during the Commercial Revolution," *AHR,* XXXVIII (1932–33), 224–6.

29. L. F. Salzman, *English Industries of the Middle Ages* (new ed.; Oxford: Clarendon Press, 1932), 88.

30. David Herlihy, *Pisa in the Early Renaissance. A Study of Urban Growth* (New Haven: Yale University Press, 1958), 144.

31. Compare the figures before 1566 with the figures after that date in Lewis, *op. cit.,* 253–5.

32. Cf. Leon Schick, *op. cit.,* 272–3, and Jacob Strieder, *Jacob Fugger the Rich,* trans. Mildred L. Hartsaugh (New York: The Adelphi Co., 1931), 32, 121.

33. J. U. Nef, "Note on the Progress of Iron Production in England, 1540–1640," *The Journal of Political Economy,* XLIV (1936), 401–3.

CHAPTER **IV**   *Banking and Finance*

M UCH OF THE progress which occurred in commerce and industry
during the Renaissance period depended on adequate financing.
Thus, expansion of international trade, enlargement of mining ventures, and the opening of new industries — all were made possible by
greater availability of money and a corresponding sophistication in
matters of finance. Indeed, tradition identifies the Renaissance with
"big banking" and the Medici or the Fuggers in the same way as it
identifies the Renaissance with the discovery of the New World or with
the inception of modern art. Although in these identifications tradition has allowed itself considerable license, there is no question that
finance during the Renaissance made considerable progress toward
modernity in spite of the persistence of hardened medieval practices.
What this progress amounted to can be seen if we examine the three
types of financial enterprises prevalent during the Renaissance, namely,
money-changing, pawnbroking, and banking.

Types of Financial Enterprises

MONEY-CHANGING Money-changing, existent since man first began
to employ money in trading operations, continued to be in high demand
during the Renaissance age because of the great variety of coinage systems still in effect. Wherever there was a fair or a business center where
merchants of several different regions congregated, money-changing
was indispensable and was performed by professional money-changers.
Located in their small booths about the market square, these clever professionals exchanged coins of one principality for coins of another, or
coins of one metal for coins of a different metal, and so facilitated commercial transactions. But important as was this function to trade operations, it was not the only role which these men played in business.

From their service as changers of money these men made profits
from advantageous fluctuations of the exchange, and with the capital

so accumulated they entered the field of finance, extending credit to merchants and municipalities. If they did not have enough of their own capital to engage in these operations, they adopted the modern practice of accepting deposits and employing the money so acquired in their own business on the assumption that all deposits were not likely to be demanded at the same time. Thus the money-changers of the Renaissance era operated as receivers of deposits, dispensers of credit, speculators in exchange, and private investors, that is, as bankers. Indeed, they were recognized as such by the state, which licensed them, determined the amount of bond they would have to post to protect the depositors against any defalcations, and defined their operations.

Some idea of this type of banking, and, incidentally, of a business partnership also, can be obtained from the following article of a partnership for the establishment of a private bank in Barcelona:

> Articles made, God willing, between the Honorable Galceran de Strelrich, Knight, and the Lady Francina, his wife, as parties of the first part; and Don Guillem Bages, merchant and citizen of Barcelona, as party of the second part.
>
> I. First, said Mossignor Galceran de Strelrich and his wife contribute in cash six hundred pounds, Barcelona, which they proposed to invest in a bank which, God willing, the same Guillem Bages is to establish in his house at the street corner in front of the slaughter house. All the gains *whether from the exchange of Florins or other coins for silver and copper* [italics added], and all the profits from the funds employed in woolen or linen cloth, fish, salt, oil, and other merchandise shall belong to said bank common to the partnership. The said Guillem promises well, loyally, and safely to rule and administer the said bank, seeking for it all the possible profits and avoiding all the dangers; keeping good, loyal and true account of all the affairs of the said bank.[1]

PAWNBROKING While money-changing served business people and travelers, pawnbroking supplied the needs of the consumers. Poor men, priests, or princes needing money could not easily secure loans from money-changers or bankers whose business interests were better served if their investments were in more liquid ventures. There was therefore a real need of a business institution that could meet the demands for consumer loans. Pawnbroking answered that need. Indeed, it was this service to the community that permitted its existence; for, though it was an open form of usury, a practice which was denounced by the church and state and resented by the public, it was nevertheless officially sanctioned as a necessary form of business. The public authorities preferred controlled usury to clandestine gouging of the unfortunate debtor.

Though licensed and publicly advertised by a sign of three golden balls, the pawnshops were usually located away from the principal business sections and off the main thoroughfares. It was good for the pawnbroker's business if the more prominent clients were able to visit his shop without the necessity of exposing themselves embarrassingly to public gaze and sharp-tongued rumor. Operated as individual or as partnership enterprises, the pawnshops extended loans for short periods, usually for less than one year. They charged interest varying from four pennies per pound per month to two pennies per pound per week, that is, from about 20 per cent to 43⅓ per cent, the maximum allowable by license, and accepted all kinds of movables as security. Evidence from a Pistoian pawnkeepers account book dated 1417 shows that the pledges accepted included "articles of clothing and apparel, tools and agricultural implements, jewelry (pearls, silver, buckles, etc.), arms and armor (sword, dagger, cross-bow, etc.), kitchenware and household utensils, and calfskins,"[2] and reveals that the customers were both commonfolk and gentry. The safe margin of loan was about 60 per cent of the value of the pledge. Pledges had to be kept for a year and could be sold thereafter if they were not redeemed. Profits, while not much higher than the 36 per cent interest legally charged by some American small loan firms, must have been substantial, for some brokers when in need of capital for expansion induced investors to make deposits with them by offering 10 per cent interest in return. To be sure there were risks, losses on loans, unexpected increases in overhead expenses, even revocations of license and confiscations of property, but in most cases the operators weathered the storms and made profit for themselves while rendering service to the community as providers of consumer credit.

Common throughout Europe, the privately operated pawnshop was in Italy supplemented by the publicly owned pawnshop, the *mons pietatis*. The first such shop was established in Perugia, about 1461, by the resident papal lieutenant. Pope Paul II gave his approval in 1467, and by 1500 there were about eighty such establishments throughout the peninsula. The rest of Europe did not have this type of pawnshop during the Renaissance period: it was not until 1618, for example, that one appeared in Belgium.

Originally, the *mons pietatis* was intended to be a charitable institution, obtaining its funds from free-will offerings, getting administrators to work without compensation, and extending loans only to the poor, free of charge. But this reliance on charity soon proved to be impracticable, and so more feasible ways of doing business were allowed to creep in. First to be admitted was the practice of charging service fees for processing the loans. This was officially approved in 1493. Then, in order to stimulate the flow of capital to the *montes*, the practice of accepting deposits and of paying interest on them — 5 per cent normally — was permitted. And when capital began to accumulate, the further step was taken of permitting business loans and of charging 8 to 10 per cent interest for them.

Thus what started out as a charitable loan institution serving the poor ended up, like the privately owned pawnshop, as a bank serving business as well as the indigent.

BANKING While money-changing and pawnbroking were forms of banking — in fact in Florence they were so called, money-changers' shops being known as *banchi in mercato,* and pawnshops as *banchi di pegno* — the more common form was that of the merchant-banker. As in the Middle Ages, the successful merchant was very likely to have some ready money and so be in a position to venture into banking. If in addition to merchandising he also engaged in profitable manufacturing and mining enterprises and thereby added to his wealth, he might really become a big banker. And if his banking ventures should prove to be profitable, he might then make banking his primary business. To illustrate this relationship between business and banking and at the same time to learn something of the banking operations of the two foremost banking houses of the Renaissance period we might turn to the Medici of Florence and the Fuggers of Augsburg.

BANKING: THE MEDICI The full picture of the Medici banking operations does not reveal itself until shortly after the middle of the fifteenth century. The Medici started out in the business world in the thirteenth century as ordinary makers of cloth. During the fourteenth century they branched out into real estate, merchandising, and exchange business; and their successes in all these lines led them to expand beyond their home base at Florence.[3] By 1458, according to the Florentine tax assessment of that year, the main branch of the family, that headed by Cosimo, had partnerships in two clothmaking concerns, in a silkmaking concern, in trading branches at Milan, Venice, Avignon, Genoa (transferred to Lyon in 1466), Bruges, and London, and an interest but not a direct partnership in a concern at Rome. In 1466 Cosimo acquired an interest in the Societas Aluminum, a mining company which secured from the pope the right to exploit the alum mines in the papal town of Tolfa. Where the Medici had no branches of their own, as at Valencia, Bologna, Genoa, Cologne, and Lubeck, they were represented by other Italian houses or by native merchants. Their business connections were therefore continental in scope.

Although all the concerns enumerated are identified with the Medici, they were actually and legally individual organizations. For one example we may turn to the branch at Bruges. In 1455 a partnership was organized with a total capital of £3,000 groat. Three members of the Medici family, Piero and Giovanni (sons of Cosimo) and Pierfrancesco, their cousin, contributed £1,900 groat; Gierozzo de' Pigli, a former manager of this branch, had £600 groat; and Agnelo Tani engaged £500 groat and agreed to manage the branch. The articles of incorporation specifically confined the business activity of this branch "to lawful trade and to licit and honorable exchange transactions." Profits, "God help," and losses, "God forbid," were to be divided in the ratio of three, one, one respectively. The manager was not allowed to expend on the purchase of English or Flemish wool more than £600 annually, and was further requested to submit reports to Florence at specified intervals. It would seem that the policy was decided at the family office in Florence and that accounting was checked there also because the greatest investors were the Medici, but it is clear that the management was in the hands of a partner-manager and not a factor and that the branch was operated actually as an independent concern. The silk-manufacturing concern may be taken as another example. Three men formed a partnership with a total capitalization of 5,000 florins. The share of Cosimo de' Medici was 4,200 florins; that of Francesco Berlinghieri, the manager, 800 florins; and that of Jacopo di Berago, his services as assistant manager. Profits were to be shared in accordance with the ratio of 60 per cent for Cosimo, 28 per cent for Francesco, and 12 per cent for Jacopo. This partnership was operated separately from the two woolen businesses or the bank in the palace.[4]

As in the early days, so at the height of their expansion, the Medici were basically merchants. They traded in wool, cloth, silk, alum, spices, wine, olive oil, and in other commodities. However, like many a medieval merchant, the Medici partnerships early engaged in traffic in bills of exchange. We may use Professor Raymond de Roover's illustration of such a transaction:

> Around July 15, 1441, the Medici of Venice bought a bill on Bruges at the rate of 54½ groats per Venetian ducat. Two months later, when the bill matured, they received in Bruges 54½ groats per each ducat. With the proceeds of this bill the Bruges branch, acting as agent for the Venice branch, bought a bill on Venice, payable at the end of two months, at the rate of 51½ groats per ducat. The Medici of Venice thus made a profit of 3 groats on each ducat over a period of four months, since they received 54½ groats and paid only 51½ groats.[5]

There were variations from this regular pattern, and sometimes unexpected risks ate up the anticipated profits, but on the whole a concern like the Medici, keeping itself well posted on economic and political affairs throughout western Europe, could make traffic in bills of exchange a profitable business.

From the articles of incorporation of the Bruges branch and of the silk partnership it can be seen that the original capital was not large and presumably insufficient for extensive operations. To overcome this shortage of capital the Medici adopted two practices. They plowed their profits back into the partnership, and they accepted deposits from the public. The deposits were not demand deposits but time deposits requiring notices of withdrawal from three to twelve months in advance. The deposits were employed at the discretion of the partnership, and in return for them the depositor could expect some interest. The average rate of interest was 10 per cent, but it was not obligatory. Like the modern income bonds, deposits with the Medici paid dividends only when they earned a profit.

Such was the famous Medici banking house. It was neither a house nor a pure banking concern, but several separate partnerships engaged in the purchase, manufacture, and sale of merchandise, and in trading in bills of exchange. Even if the Medici accepted deposits to supplement their own capital, which in 1451 amounted to only 88,269 florins, neither their financial resources — Cosimo at his death was worth 235,137 florins — nor their transactions appear to have been overwhelming.[6] In England, poor management on the part of the local representatives and losses incurred as a result of loans to the king and some nobles who later suffered in the War of Roses led to a deficit of 51,553 florins and forced the closing of the London branch (1478).[7] Likewise an uncollectable loan of £9,500 groat to Charles of Burgundy and the loss of two galleys which the Bruges partnership operated brought that concern on the rocks. This is not world-shaking finance.

BANKING: THE FUGGERS Like the Medici the Fuggers had their start as weavers of cloth. Hans Fugger moved to Augsburg about 1380 and, as weaver and trader in fustian, accumulated a small fortune of 3,000 florins. One of his sons, Jakob I, gained recognition as master of the gild of weavers, and together with his brothers expanded merchandising to include transactions in spices, velvets, and silk. Under his three sons, Ulrich, George, and Jakob II who gave up a prebend in order first to study business as an apprentice in Venice and then to join in the management of the family interests, the concern was reorganized in 1494 as a partnership, with Ulrich contributing 21,656 florins, George, 17,177, and Jakob, 15,552. The terms of incorporation also provided for the preservation of the bulk of the capital in the company in the event of death or separation of its members or their heirs, for the retention of the management in the hands of the oldest male members, and for the apprenticeship of their heirs to those in charge. In this way the firm's working capital was perpetuated in business without serious depletion of resources, and the management was freed from the evils of divided or contending business counsels. Under these arrangements the company expanded its operations into other fields of business — particularly exchange, banking, and mining — and prospered mightily.

Even before its reorganization in 1457 the company had secured an interest in mining. In return for loans of 23,677 florins and of 150,000 florins to Duke Sigismund of Tyrol, the company acquired, at a price below the free-market price and until the debt and the interest were liquidated, the Duke's share of the mineral output of the Schwaz silver and copper mines. Similar but more numerous and more extensive rights were secured from the extravagant Emperor Maximilian I. At the same time, in order to protect their interests in the Tyrolese mining against the competing Hungarian silver and copper, and possibly also to secure a copper cartel for Europe, they joined forces with the famous house of Thurzo, a family of mining engineers from Cracow, who secured from King Matthias Corvinus profitable mining rights in Hungary and who were in need of capital. With the profits realized from the control of these mining operations in central Europe and from the supplementary earnings from merchandising and exchange, the Fuggers established themselves as the foremost financiers on the continent. Their great resources and the soundness of their credit made it possible for them to get the lion's share of the financing (543,000 florins out of a total of 850,000 florins) necessary to buy the votes of the Electors for the future Emperor Charles V; and with Charles on the throne, the Fuggers naturally extended their operations throughout his far-flung dominions. In return for loans to the new Emperor, they secured contracts to work the quicksilver mines of Almaden in Spain and the silver mines of Guadalcanal, as well as leases on the royal revenues from the properties of the nationalized religious military orders of Santiago, Calatrava, and Alcantara. All these operations made for spectacular growth of the firm. Properties and business assets which in 1511 amounted to 196,791 florins snowballed into 2,032,652 florins by 1527, a year after Jakob II's death, while the prestige of the firm grew to great heights. In the words of a contemporary

> The names of Jacob Fugger and of his nephews are known in all the kingdoms and countries and even in pagan lands. Emperors, kings, princes and nobles have sent ambassadors to them, the pope has greeted and embraced them as very dear sons, and cardinals have stood up before them.[8]

For the next two decades the firm under the guiding hand of Jakob's nephew Anton continued to grow and prosper. Agencies and factories were added until the long arm of the Fugger concern extended from Lisbon to Danzig and from Danzig to Italy; the Thurzo were "dumped" but their interests in Hungarian mines retained; and the assets more than doubled, rising to about five million florins by 1546. But great as was their economic power, the Fuggers failed within one hundred years after this high point. In the first place, they found it impossible to compete with the influx of cheap treasure from the New World, which grew steadily after 1550; and since they had much of their capital tied up in continental mining enterprises, they naturally suffered in profits and in credit. In the second place, they had tied their fortunes to the rising Habsburg star; and as long as the Habsburg star was ascending, their business prospered. But once the star began to drop, as it did under Ferdinand of Austria and Philip II of Spain, bankruptcy was inevitable. Unable to collect some eight million florins from the failing Habsburgs, the Fuggers lost their credit and their business.[9]

These two financial houses have been chosen to illustrate the point that in the Renaissance times big banking was a by-product of merchandising and of manufacturing. Hence where there were successful merchants there were likely to be bankers. London, Paris, Lyon, Cahors, Bruges, Ghent, Arras, Antwerp, Venice, Genoa, Florence, Barcelona, Lisbon, Nuremberg, and many other commercial centers had their merchants who dealt in letters of exchange, made loans, collected interest, and even accepted deposits. Beginning with the late 1200's and continuing through the Renaissance, scores of wealthy merchant families and partnerships engaged in exactly the same type of banking as a by-product of trade and manufacturing. Florence had its Frescobaldi, Bardi, Peruzzi, Acciajuoli, Buonaccorsi, Mozzi, Portinari, Gualterati, Pazzi, Capponi, Strozzi, Mozzi; Lucca had its Riccardi; Piacenza had its Scotti; Siena had its Chigi; Genoa had its Centurioni, Guistiniani, Spinola, and Grimaldi; Barcelona had its Peres des Caus and Andreus d'Olivella; Paris had its Marcels and Dampmartins and the notorious Coeur and Remy; Arras had its Louchards and Crespins; London had its de la Poles, Pultneys, and Whittingtons; Augsburg had its Welsers, Imhofs, and Hochstetters; and so on.

STATE BANKS Although most of the banking was of the form described above, there were banks which had their origin in state action. Faced with the need for ready cash, the governments of Venice and of Genoa collected forced loans from wealthy citizens and in return assigned to these creditors certain state revenues with interest and allowed them to issue negotiable certificates covering the amount of the loan. These creditors were organized as banks, in Venice under the name of Bank of St. Mark, and in Genoa as the Bank of St. George,[10] and were granted the privilege of accepting deposits. These two banks, usually considered as state banks, were really private banks which handled the funded debt of the respective states. Even the Bank of Barcelona, the Taula di Camba, founded in January, 1401, and generally regarded as a true state bank because its credit resources were by regulation reserved to the exclusive use of the city, did not absolutely reserve its functions to the state only. There are records of accounts which reveal overdrafts by private individuals, that is, in reality, loans to private parties.[11]

MEDIEVAL ORIGINS OF "BANKING" Although these four types of "banking" have been presented as prevalent during the Renaissance, it should not be assumed that they all originated in that age.[12] Money-changers as changers and as lenders were both indispensable and numerous for centuries before the Renaissance. The same applies to pawn-brokers. Big merchants as bankers appear in the late Middle Ages. William Cade of Saint-Omer was making extensive loans to Henry II of England as early as the 1160's; in the following century the Crespins of Arras were helping to finance the needs of the Count of Flanders and of several Flemish towns to the extent of 200,000 li. par.; the Florentine wool merchants, Bardi and Peruzzi, advanced such vast sums to Edward III to meet the costs of his wars that they went bankrupt when he defaulted; and Géraud Gayte, merchant of Clermont and Philip V's treasurer, lent Philip (1316–1322) about 460,000 li. tur.[13] Only the so-called state banks, if we except that of Genoa which had its inception in 1157 and its incorporation in 1318, were new in the Renaissance.

Hence, for the most part, the banking systems of Renaissance were direct continuations from the Middle Ages. What differences existed were few. The amounts of money handled in the Renaissance were greater, largely because of the insatiable demands of large-scale warfare; the preponderance of the two large houses in the Renaissance, the Medici and the Fuggers, was not matched in the preceding age; and, as we shall presently see, transactions in state bonds and in other paper as well as in commodities, and the accompanying penchant for speculation,[14] gained a more dominant position in Renaissance banking than they had in medieval banking.

The Bourse or Exchange

DEFINITION AND ORIGIN OF EXCHANGE According to the late Professor Ehrenberg, the exchange or bourse, to call it by its continental name, "is an assembly meeting at frequent intervals, usually daily, consisting of the merchants and other persons, who meet for the purpose of dealing without exhibiting, delivering, and paying for their goods at the same time."[15] It grew out of the medieval and Renaissance fairs. But whereas the fairs were usually open from two to four weeks only once or twice a year, the bourse operated throughout the entire year. Also, whereas the merchants had their goods with them at the fairs, they did not have to bring them to the bourse but could get by either with samples or merely on their business reputation. These changes could take place only if the supply of goods was greater than could be disposed of at the interrupted fairs and if the goods were becoming standardized. The bourse then is something like the modern commodity exchange, where merchants assemble to buy and sell commodities sight-unseen to be delivered in the future.

Associated with this exchange in commodities, there was another exchange where merchants and bankers met to deal in money and credit, sometimes to meet the obligations they assumed at the commodity exchange, and sometimes as entirely independent transactions. This also was an outgrowth of the fairs. The greater fairs, it should be remembered, usually set aside several days at the end of each session to enable the merchants to settle their accounts in a kind of "clearing-house" operation. If this operation were separated from the fair and conducted the year round and if it also included traffic in bills and securities independent of transactions on the commodity exchange, we would then have the second exchange. This is what apparently happened, as is evidenced by the fact that the "payment" operations of the fairs at Bergen-op-Zoom were transferred to Antwerp but not the trading operations.

Naturally, where great numbers of international merchants assembled to buy and sell commodities, an exchange was likely to develop. Hence by the middle of the sixteenth century there were exchanges at Bologna, Florence, Genoa, Lucca, Milan, Venice, Rome, Naples, Palermo, Nuremberg, Augsburg, Francfort-on-the-Main, Antwerp, Rouen, Paris, Besançon, Lyon, Seville, and Saragossa. In the next half-century some others appeared, for example, London, founded in 1571 by Queen Elizabeth's financier Sir Thomas Gresham, Hamburg, and Amsterdam. Not all of these were at the same stage of development, some remained in an embryonic stage and were small, while others were fast attaining maturity and growing in importance. Of the latter, two attained great prominence, namely, those of Antwerp and Lyon.

THE ANTWERP BOURSE The Antwerp bourse owed its origin to the pre-eminence of the city as an entrepot, after Bruges, its medieval predecessor, had declined because of the rigid protectionist policy of Flanders where Bruges was located — Flanders banned English cloth after England (in the fourteenth century) shifted from the export of raw wool to the manufacture and export of woolen cloth — because of the silting of the harbor at Sluys, and because Emperor Maximilian, to punish Bruges for its rebellion in 1488, transferred the staple to Antwerp. About the same time, the municipal authorities of Antwerp permitted year-round marketing (1484) and the Portuguese selected it as the distributing center for their spice trade (1501). Hence all western Europe began to flock there to engage in trade, and soon it became the chief center for the distribution of English woolens, Flemish and Brabantine linen, Baltic wax and timber, southern German fustian and copper, Portuguese spices and sugar, and Italian silks and alum.[16] This large-scale commodity trade naturally required some provision for credit operations and so a "new bourse" was established about the turn of the century. These developments happened to coincide with the rise of the

Habsburg political star. To promote their international interests the emperors needed an unending supply of money. They naturally turned to the merchants at Antwerp, and their constant borrowing made the bourse a great money market. The end result of this development may be described in the words of a contemporary merchant-banker, Ludovico Guicciardini, brother of the famous Italian historian, as they appear in his *Description of the Low Countries*.

> The merchants go morning and evening at a certain time to the Bourse of the English, the merchant bourse. There they do business with the help of brokers of every language, who are there in great numbers, chiefly as to buying and selling of commodities of every kind. Then they go to the new bourse where in the same way they deal chiefly in bills and money loans.[17]

As Guicciardini reports, one business operation on this double exchange was the sale and purchase of commodities. Out of this operation, and because the great concourse of merchants made it possible to discover what commodities were short and what were long, emerged the practice of speculation in commodities. A wool merchant, for example, discerning possibilities of making profit in pepper, may put an order for several sacks to be delivered at some future date. He might wait and accept delivery, or, if he changed his mind in the meantime, he might sell his order to some other party. Hence, instead of a regular transaction, his became purely speculative. Another regular type of operation was the sale and purchase of bills of exchange. But out of this developed the practice of speculating on the rate of exchange. It began as wagers between dealers in exchange that the rate will be this figure or that, but in order to win the wager one or the other dealer, or both, might try to influence the market by buying or selling large orders in bills as they thought their chances of profit demanded. When this practice became widespread the result was speculation on the rate of exchange. The same kind of speculation appeared in connection with fluctuations of commodity prices. Wagers were offered that copper prices, for example, would drop in the next eight weeks, and so on. But perhaps the greatest operation was that in loans. Kings, principalities, and cities in need of money negotiated large loans from merchant firms and offered bonds as security. The loans were usually short-term loans and the interest was high, sometimes up to 20 per cent or more. To obtain the necessary capital the merchant lenders, with better credit rating that that of the kings, in turn borrowed from others, or they raised it by selling shares in the loans to small investors. Also, large firms like the Fuggers or the Welsers sometimes found it necessary to borrow. Finally, the bonds were themselves put on the market. The result of all this was a vast money market which made Antwerp the Wall Street of the sixteenth century.[18]

THE BOURSE AT LYON The bourse at Lyon, second only to Antwerp, was an outgrowth of the free fairs established there in the fifteenth century. The city had enjoyed a remarkable commercial growth in the thirteenth and the early fourteenth centuries, as witnessed by the international operations of one of its greatest merchants, Ponce of Lyon, but its business dropped drastically thereafter and it fell into a desperate economic plight. It was in the midst of this depression that the city's interests and the interests of the future Charles VII coincided: the city was eager to overcome the depression, and the Dauphin, barred from the northern financial centers by the Anglo-Burgundian occupation of northern France, was anxious to find a new source of money. Both parties felt that the solution might be found in the establishment of fairs in the city. Accordingly, after some earnest pleas by the citizens, Charles granted to Lyon, on February 9, 1420, the right to hold two free fairs. He gave it further support in 1445 by permitting the opening of a third fair and by trying to divert more business to the city by forbidding the French merchants to attend the fairs of Geneva whither much of European commerce and finance had moved during the Hundred Years' War. With these favorable provisions to promote them and with the restoration of peace, the fairs developed rapidly. They were further aided by the establishment of Jacques Coeur's extensive business enterprises in the city and by the actions of Louis XI. On October 20, 1462, Louis confirmed the three fairs, reasserted his father's prohibition, and added a new ban denying to foreign merchants the right of transit across France to Geneva. In the following year, on March 8, he authorized a fourth fair and specifically permitted the merchants at Lyon to hold a *banc de change public*. Under such patronage the fairs grew, drew unto themselves many merchants from Nuremberg, Geneva, Lucca,

Florence, Genoa, Milan, and raised Lyon into an international commercial center. A large volume of business was transacted, and to facilitate payments a "clearing house" was established where, after each fair, the merchants assembled to settle their accounts. Normally, the excess debits were not paid in cash but were settled by bills payable at the next or at some subsequent fair. Often these notes were sold; and so, in addition to merchandise, money bills entered the stream of business transactions. To these transactions was soon added the business of supplying loans to the French kings. Francis I's great demands for money attracted additional merchant-financiers to Lyon, and it became, after Antwerp, the largest European market for money. Like the promissory bills and the customary bills of exchange, royal bonds were sold and bought. The fairs thus gave birth to a real bourse.[19]

Altogether, the extent of its operations was commanding. The Venetian ambassador Navagero, as early as 1528, saw in it "the foundation of Italian commerce and in great part of the commerce of Spain and Flanders"; while some sixty-eight years later the merchants of St. Gall revealed considerable surprise at the volume of business "cleared" through the bourse and the method of doing it. Said they

> It is well known that the vast business which is done there, either in banking, or in merchandising transactions, is conducted through notes and securities which are passed there. In such a fair there will be transactions worth a million in gold, and yet, among all those participating in them, not 10,000 *écus* will have changed hands.[20]

State Financing[21]

Significant as were these advances in the world of finance, they can be presumed to have had some effect on the methods of financing state needs. However, as will be shown presently, the resulting changes were not as extensive as might be expected.

In the first century of the Renaissance, the states met their urgent financial needs as they did during the Middle Ages. Aside from increasing old taxes and devising new ones and improving their tax systems, they had to resort to various forms of borrowing, and these did not change substantially from the medieval forms of borrowing. In general, the states secured short-term loans from merchant bankers, native or foreign, on the security of some royal property or some fiscal rights and at high rates of interest; sometimes they borrowed from their own officials and towns, occasionally even under duress; and in some instances, particularly in the Netherlands and in Germany, they sold annuities either directly or mediately through some towns whose credit rating was better than their own. Thus, just as the Riccardi of Lucca, between 1272 and 1294, lent Edward I of England some £392,000 and in return had the right to collect all the customs revenue, or just as the Bardi of Florence advanced 10,000 ounces of gold in 1300 to the Angevin ruler of Naples and in return received all rights to the income from export duties and from the tax on salt and on the sale of Saracen slaves, so, about a century and a half later, as reported above, the Fuggers made two separate loans of 23,677 florins and 150,000 florins to the Duke of Tyrol and received the rights to his share of the output of the Schwaz silver and copper mines. Likewise, just as Philip V (1316–1322) of France secured some 460,000 *li. tur.* from Gayte, head of his *Chambre des comptes*, so about a century later Emperor Sigismund I and his son-in-law Albert II borrowed 40,000 gulden from Sigismund's *camerarius,* Konrad von Weinsberg, and so in 1450 Charles VII got 100,000 *écus* from his *argentier*, the notorious Jacques Coeur. Similarly, just as Count Guy (1287–1300) of Flanders borrowed from Arras, Bruges, and Ypres, so Philip VI (1328–1350) raised money from Amiens and Louis XI (1461–1483) from Lyon and other towns. Finally, just as the Count of Holland in the 1330's was raising money by selling annuities, so Philip the Good of Burgundy was doing the same 120 years later.[22] Such examples can be multiplied many times over, and they would all show that the medieval methods of financing state needs persisted throughout the Renaissance period.

Later in the course of the Renaissance period, as the states grew larger and their governments and international wars more costly and the need for money mounted, the old methods of raising revenue had to be expanded and new ones discovered.

For an example of the expansion of an old method, we might turn to France and its celebrated Renaissance sovereign Francis I whose luxurious court life and ambitious foreign policy imposed impossible demands on the treasury and required the maximum exploitation of all sources of income. One of the readiest sources was, of course, the reviving towns, and so Francis turned to them. In 1522 his government ceded to Paris, on condition of the right of repurchase, the royal rights to certain imposts in the city. To raise the funds necessary for the purchase price, the city sold bonds to private subscribers and turned the receipts over to the king. And to encourage subscriptions, the city put up as surety the anticipated revenues from these ceded imposts and declared the bonds transferable. The same practice was repeated in 1536–1537 in many cities throughout the country. At Lyon, for example, certain royal imposts were sold outright to the town for the sum of 84,732 *livres*. Since the king needed money urgently, he got the city to give him 35,000 *livres* in advance, which the city raised by negotiating short-term loans at 4 per cent per quarter. But to finance the entire transaction the city sold bonds payable in two semiannual installments and bearing 10 per cent interest. Five years elapsed before enough bonds were sold to discharge the purchase price, but by that time eighty-eight subscribers had contributed 85,391 *livres*. The bonds were guaranteed by the allocation of specified tax revenues and were negotiable.[23]

Francis' method of raising money from the towns had little in it which was new, as it was quite similar to that employed by his Capetian predecessors and by the rulers of Flanders in the later Middle Ages — namely, getting advances from the towns on the security of royal revenues due from the towns and the towns finding the money by borrowing or by selling annuities. What is different is the increase in the number of towns involved in this revenue-raising measure, the frequency with which this method was employed, the relative shortness of the bond periods, and the negotiability of the bonds. In the end, this was tantamount to the king's selling royal bonds to his subjects, not directly, but mediately through the towns.

As an illustration of a new method of raising money in the Renaissance period, we might turn to Florence, which resorted to the establishment of a permanent funded debt. By 1345 the Florentine government had incurred such heavy debts that it could not even meet the regular interest payments. Some new sources of revenue had to be found, and one of these proved to be the sale of "government bonds." The purchaser paid cash for the bonds, and in return the government agreed to pay him annual dividends at a stipulated rate and to redeem the bonds within a given period of time. As surety the government earmarked certain revenues or a portion thereof, depending on the amount of bonds that were offered for sale. Thus the state acquired some additional funds, and the citizens were presented with an opportunity to invest their capital at attractive returns. This state debt the Florentines called the *monte commune*.

Promising as this system of raising money was, it still proved to be inadequate in the late fourteenth and the early fifteenth centuries as the city's wars multiplied and grew more expensive. Hence, still another way of raising money had to be devised — the sale of dowry insurance by the state. The fathers were encouraged to buy time insurance from the state payable in full when their daughters reached their marriageable age, generally after their fifteenth year. The receipts of these sales were set up as a fund, called the dowry fund (*monte delle doti*), and the state drew upon it to meet some of its expenses, just like banks today make use of demand deposits in their banking operations. If it tapped the fund so much that the reserve fell below the claims, then it offered the subscribers only a percentage of the face value of the policy and charged the balance to the fund, payable at some future date at an interest rate sufficiently attractive to make the deferment acceptable.

With the two funds operating at the same time, the state sometimes encouraged the holders of the *monte commune* bonds to exchange these, at stipulated rates, for bonds of the dowry fund. In that way the state secured postponement of redemption of the first bonds for several years and the holders saw their investments earning interest, usually higher than the interest on the *monte commune* bonds, over a longer period of time.[24]

The methods which France and Florence devised to finance their needs were adopted by other towns and countries.[25] And the result of the adoption of these methods was a partial transformation of state financing. In addition to the standard medieval practices of procuring short-term loans, of "farming" the imposts, and of getting subscriptions from towns, the governments had recourse to the sale of bonds and to the creation of funded debt.

Summary

No Medici and no Fuggers in the Middle Ages; no state banks; no commodity or financial exchanges; no formal speculation in market prices or in public bonds. But all these appeared in the era of the Renaissance. Viewed thus, it would seem that an actual revolution in finance had occurred during the Renaissance. On the other hand, the Medici and the Fuggers were anticipated by many lesser but nevertheless great merchant-bankers, while money-changing and pawnbroking as forms of banking were the same in both ages. As to commodity and financial exchanges, these did not arise until the early sixteenth century and so they had no effect on business during most of the Renaissance period, which, until the 1500's, had to depend, like the later Middle Ages, on the great fairs and on the "clearing-house" operations at the end of these fairs. Finally, formal speculation on the exchanges had its medieval counterpart in the money-changer's informal speculation in the exchange of species and in the merchant's speculation in the purchase and sale of bills of exchange. Viewed thus, what passes for a revolution during the Renaissance appears less of an actual revolution and more like the preparation of a seedbed for a revolution soon to take place.

1. Taken from A. P. Usher, *The Early History of Deposit Banking in Mediterranean Europe,* 251. The rest of the document is very informative and deserves to be read.

2. Raymond de Roover, *Money, Banking and Credit in Mediaeval Bruges,* 121.

3. On this early period of their enterprise see Gene A. Brucker, "The Medici in the Fourteenth Century," *Speculum,* XXXII (1957), 1–26.

4. For these two examples see Raymond de Roover, *The Medici Bank, Its Organization, Management, Operations, and Decline* (New York: New York University Press, 1948), 14–18, 28–29.

5. *Ibid.,* 35–36.

6. On the deposits see *ibid.,* 26, n. 74; on Cosimo's estate see Gertrude Randolph Bramlette Richards (ed.), *Florentine Merchants in the Age of the Medici* (Cambridge: Harvard University Press, 1932), 47; and on the Medici capital see R. de Roover's chapter in *CEcH,* III (1963), 83–84.

7. Mallett, *op. cit.,* 252–3.

8. Quoted from Henri Hauser and Augustine Renaudet, *Les débuts de l'age moderne,* vol. VIII of *Peuples et civilizations, histoire générale,* ed. by L. Halphen and Ph. Sagnac (3d ed.; Paris: Presses universitaires de France, 1946), 350.

9. For an account of the financial operations of the Fuggers consult Richard Ehrenberg, *Capital and Finance in the Age of the Renaissance, A Study of the Fuggers and their Connections,* trans. H. M. Lucas (New York: Harcourt, Brace and Co., 1928), 64–132. For a more detailed account of the operations of Jacob Fugger see Leon Schick, *op. cit.*

10. On the Bank of St. George, its origins out of the fiscal plight of the city, its financial operations, and its role in the administration of the city as a counterpart of the civic organs of government see Heers, *Gênes au xvᵉ siècle,* 97–146 and tables VI, VII, VIII, at the end of book.

11. Usher, *op. cit.,* 271–2, 331–7.

12. On medieval origins of banking see R. de Roover's chapter "Bank Deposits as Money" in his *Money, Banking and Credit in Mediaeval Bruges,* where he points out that deposit banking was well developed in Italy by 1200 and in Flanders by 1300 (247–8); and André–E. Sayous, "Les opérations des banquiers Italiens en Italie et aux foires de Champagne pendant le xiiiᵉ siècle," *Revue historique,* CLXX (1932), 1–31.

13. For these and other medieval merchant-bankers see *CEcH,* III, 452–60, 474–81, 493–8, 538.

14. Ehrenberg, *op. cit.,* 239ff. and 325–8.

15. *Ibid.,* 54.

16. On the rise of Antwerp and its role as an entrepot see V. Vazquez de Prada, *Lettres marchandes d'Anvers, École pratique des hautes études — VIᵉ section, Centre de recherches historiques, Affaires et gens d'affaires,* XV (Paris: S.E.V.P.E.N., no date), I, 22–34, 67–109, 151–64.

17. Cited from James Bruce Ross and Mary Martin McLaughlin, *The Portable Renaissance Reader* (New York: The Viking Press, 1953), 192. For a recent account of the genesis of the bourse see E. de Coornaert, "Les bourses d'Anvers aux xvᵉ et xviᵉ siècles," *Revue historique,* CCXVII (1957), 20–28.

18. For a more detailed account of all these operations see Ehrenberg, *op. cit.,* 233–50, and his chapters on the Fuggers and other financiers.

19. On the fairs of Lyon see Marc Brésard, *Les foires de Lyon au xvᵉ et xviᵉ siècles* (Paris: Auguste Picard, 1914), and Usher, *op. cit.,* 120–5. For an informative recent treatment of the exchange transactions at Lyon, with data taken from primary sources, see Gioffre, *op. cit.,* 97–113.

20. Both citations taken from Hauser and Renaudet, *op. cit.,* 347–8.

21. A valuable introductory study is to be found in Usher, *op. cit.,* chap. 5, "Long Term Lending and Public Debts."

22. For these and other examples see *CEcH,* III, 430–533, *passim.* Also cf. Usher, *op. cit.,* 344–86 on the funded debt of Barcelona.

23. For these examples see Roger Doucet, *Finances municipales et crédit public à Lyon au xvie siècle* (Paris: Librairie des sciences économiques et sociales, 1937), 6–16. For comparison of how Catalonia financed its operations see Usher, *op. cit.,* 410–32.

24. On the Florentine *monte* see L. F. Marks, "The Financial Oligarchy in Florence under Lorenzo," *Italian Renaissance Studies, a Tribute to the late Cecilia M. Ady,* ed. E. F. Jacob (London: Faber and Faber, 1960), 123–47.

25. By Germany, for example; cf. F. Braudel, "Les emprunts de Charles-Quint sur la place d'Anvers," *Charles-Quint et son temps. Colloques internationaux du centre national de la recherche scientifique* [hereinafter to be cited as *Charles-Quint et son temps*] (Paris: Editions du centre national de la recherche scientifique, 1959), 191–201.

V The Role of the State in the Economic Life of the Renaissance and Economic Theory

The Role of the State in the Economic Life of the Renaissance

IN THE Middle Ages, following the collapse of the Carolingian empire, commerce and industry in western Europe were in general controlled locally, by the feudal lords in their domains, and by the municipal governments and gilds in the chartered towns. However, from the eleventh century on, as monarchic rule became more effective, state-wide regulations began to appear, and by the thirteenth century they were quite common. Thereafter the trend grew steadily until it reached its developed form in the mercantilism of the seventeenth century.[1]

Naturally, the reasons for this intrusion of the states into the economic life of their people differed from place to place and from time to time. Still, there were some reasons which were more or less general. Thus because all states assumed responsibility for their people's welfare, most of them regulated the grain trade in time of need to ensure sufficient food supplies, defined prices and standards of quality to protect the consumer from price gouging and from inferior goods, imposed import duties on foreign manufacturers to protect domestic industry, and safeguarded the ordinary craftsmen from unfair competition of monopolists. Again, when the interests of the states required the establishment of new industries in their territories, the states invited foreign artisans to set up these industries and granted them various privileges, such as, exemption from taxation and from military service, but sometimes even the rights of monopoly. Then, because the economic theory of the day insisted that national welfare was enhanced by the availability of precious metals in the nation, many states had regulations promoting mining within their territories and banning imports of luxury goods which were normally paid for in bullion. Sometimes, when revenue needs became extreme, the states began to regulate some phases of economy simply to increase the tax intake or to facilitate the collection of taxes. Finally, on occasion, some states enacted punitive economic measures to strike against their enemies, domestic or foreign. In Flanders and Brabant, for example, the counts authorized the establishment of cloth industry in the countryside to break the power of the larger cities which generally opposed the growth of princely authority. In sum, for one reason or another, the medieval and the Renaissance states engaged increasingly in various forms of economic regulation.

The medieval examples are numerous and quite significant. Henry II of England and St. Louis of France began to control coinage by requiring that the royal issues be accepted as legal tender in all their lands.[2] St. Louis of France began asserting royal control of industry by ordering the compilation of the *Livre de métiers* which outlined the rules of trade and industry for the crafts and defined their obligations to the crown. Edward I of England established the national customs system in the hope of increasing state revenues. Aragon enacted legislation to promote the shipping industry as early as 1227, while Venice formulated the bases of its navigation policies in the famous Statuti Nautici passed between 1229 and 1255. Moreover, Venice actually intensified its control, for after nearly a century of experimenting with several different systems for organizing its merchant marine for voyages to Greece, Levant, Africa, Spain, and England, it finally decided, by 1330, on strong state control — the ships were to be owned by the state but operated by private lessees under strict government regulations.[3] Alfonso the Learned of Castile "brought all the shepherds of Castile into . . . the Honorable Assembly of the Mesta of the Shepherds"[4] and he did so with the view of improving the national treasury's chance of taxing the industry. Medieval Portuguese sovereigns, themselves producers of commodities for sale and owners of ships, regularly enacted laws and took other measures to promote international commerce and the development of a merchant marine, as did the rulers of France and England.[5] Sales of salt in France, locally controlled until 1331, became thereafter a royal monopoly. Wholesale merchants purchased it at royal storehouses, paid the *gabelle* (salt tax), and sold it to spicers and druggists who then retailed it. The export of grain in the kingdom of Naples was under strict government control, as much of its revenue came from an export duty on grain; and records of this control go back to the late Middle Ages.[6] Control of export and import trade as an instrument of foreign policy became a fine, albeit unsuccessful, art under Edward I of England who used it to erect a wall of allies around France.[7] Prices, normally under the control of gild and municipal authorities, were from time to time regulated and enforced by the state as a whole. In Castile, for example, the "cortes of 1351, 1369, and 1373 set maximum prices for barley, rye, wheat, and wine."[8] In England in 1354, the assize of wine fixed the retail prices of wine for different sections of the country. The establishment of an English wool staple, whereby English wool exporters had to assemble their wool at one place in order that the crown could the more readily collect its customs and use the wool trade more effectively as an instrument in foreign policy, began with Edward II and Edward III; while the establishment of Dordrecht as a staple town in Holland was pushed by the counts of Holland from 1294 for many decades.[9] In order to control labor, which sought to take advantage of labor shortage following the Great Plague, England enacted the famous Ordinance of Labourers in 1351 and in the same year John of France issued a proclamation which subjected Paris gilds to royal supervision.[10] Finally, it is a recognized fact, as is so clearly manifest from the shipping policies which Venice developed, that the Republic existed for commerce and commerce existed for the Republic.

Well established by the end of the Middle Ages, governmental control of economy kept pace with the growth of the Renaissance state. In France, the Edicts of Louis XI in 1479, of Henry III in 1581, and of Henry IV in 1597 were enacted with the view of extending a manageable craft-gild system to the entire country for the benefit of the nation and the king's treasury. We have also seen that state action was taken by Charles VII and Louis XI to promote Lyon as a national money market and Poitiers as a cloth-manufacturing center. In England, poor law legislation[11] and the famous Statute of Artificers of 1563 which set up controls over prices, wages, and industrial organization were national efforts to cope with the grave nationwide problem of unemployment and the concomittant social evils of idleness and vagrancy. Earlier, Henry VII took action against Venice to win free navigation for the English merchants in the Mediterranean. Spain, striving to repair the damage that befell its economy during the "Century of Troubles," launched into state control of the nation's business life on a large scale.[12] In 1484 it invited Flemish and Italian artisans to establish their crafts in Spain and offered them a ten-year tax exemption as inducement. In 1486 a ban was imposed on the importation of foreign cloth into Murcia to protect the old cloth industry there; likewise, in 1500, Neopolitan silk thread was banned from Granada in the interest of the silk industry in that province. Alfonso the Learned's regulations of the Mesta were revised in 1492 and again in 1511 to subject the sheep industry to more effective state control and, incidentally, to bring more revenue to the treasury. To restore confidence in the royal coinage, Isabella banned the private chartered mints — there were more than 150 of them at her accession — and replaced them by six state mints. When the New World was opened to trade, the Spanish crown established the famous Casa de Contratacion in 1503 which controlled all exports and imports. Portugal did the same in connection with the spice trade originating in the East Indies — in fact it was a crown monopoly. Although the kings generally sold the right to trade to syndicates, the officers of the Casa de India had the right to interfere, to fix rules and prices. Florence, Genoa, and Milan had numerous enactments restricting or banning the import of "foreign" cloth, both wool and silk, into their respective territories. Moreover, Florence, like Venice, once it inaugurated its overseas trade with England and Flanders in 1425, prescribed meticulously the itinerary of the state galleys and the manner in which the trade was to be conducted. In the Low Countries, the importation of alum became a government monopoly. In the Scandinavian lands and in Poland repeated measures were enacted to strengthen the economic role of their own nationals and to weaken that of the German Hansa. Finally, all states took action to promote new industries; and the armaments industries, particularly the manufacture of saltpeter and gunpowder, were often royal monopolies. Thus, what had started as a substantial trend during the Middle Ages became a rush in the Renaissance. Mercantilism was just around the corner.

Extensive as was this trend toward statism there were two matters closely tied to commerce that defied control. One of these was the profusion of tolls which the states were unable to eliminate. In France attempts to reduce the number of stations were "as old as the monarchy itself," but in spite of the innumerable ordinances which were issued from the fourteenth century until the day of Colbert, the state was unable to rid the nation of the incubus. Where in the fourteenth century the tolls on the Loire, between Roanne and Nantes, numbered some seventy-four, after 1437, when by royal decree all toll stations established within the last sixty years were canceled, the number had grown to 130, and as late as 1567, including the tolls on its tributaries, there were still about 120 stations. In England private tolls were all but eliminated, but the numerous town tolls "showed no tendency to disappear after the end of the Middle Ages."[13] The other matter in which statism was no more successful in the Renaissance period than during the Middle Ages was that of the uniformity of weights and measures. William Harrison's lament "that one general measure is not in use throughout England, but every market town hath in manner a several bushel"[14] reveals the failure of Tudor government to secure the desired uniformity. In France, one of the first attempts to establish standard weights and measures was made in 1321. From that time on through the reign of Francis I and until the end of the Renaissance, similar attempts were made but without notable success. French units of weight and measure knew no more uniformity in the time of the Renaissance than in the Middle Ages.

Economic Theory during the Renaissance

FACTORS UNDERLYING ECONOMIC THEORY Our survey of Renaissance economy revealed that the great majority of the people made their living as peasant farmers or as ordinary craftsmen. Hence, except for a relatively small minority, society in general lived from hand to mouth. In such a marginal standard of living any disturbance in the normal pattern of economy was likely to bring distress. Sharp trade practices, such as cornering the market of some commodity in order to force prices up, were bound to hurt those whose margin between tolerable living standards and want was very slight, and the number of people in this category was legion. For the good of society, then, economic theory had to be based, at least to some extent, on principles that took the welfare of the great majority into consideration.

Another factor which led to the same philosophy was the fact that Renaissance society, like that of the Middle Ages, still accepted the principle, philosophically at least, that man's highest goal was salvation and that mundane affairs were to be conducted in such a manner as not to jeopardize the goal. Moral values therefore were recognized as guides in the conduct of economic enterprises. Since morality opposed exploitation of one's fellow man, it followed that social and moral interests worked toward the same end and shared in the formation of a common economic theory.

Lastly, Renaissance society still accepted the church as the arbiter of what was socially and morally right. It was bound, therefore, to heed, at least in principle, the church's teaching "Whatsoever ye would that men should do to you, do ye even so to them."

What is evident from the above is that the Renaissance economic theory could not be an explanation of the ways the economy functioned, and that it was bound to be a statement of principles which certain social, moral, and religious teachings imposed on economic activities. What these principles were can be discovered by an examination of the main components of the theory, namely, the functionalism of the social classes, usury, and just price.

FUNCTIONALISM OF CLASSES From the time of the ancient philosophers tradition accepted the theory that society was so ordered that some should govern, others fight, and still others work. Man looked about him and saw that this was so, and concluded that indeed it could not be otherwise. In the Middle Ages, this class functionalism became even more obvious. Nobility and clerical hierarchy governed, knighthood fought in behalf of society, and the commoners worked. If every class fulfilled its "calling," society then sustained itself and remained orderly. But should any one class neglect its proper task, then social order would be disrupted and suffering would ensue. Moreover, in a subsistence economy if only a small fraction abandoned its task, particularly those among the commoners, the result would tend to be the same. Hence arose the notions that people should perform the tasks nature allotted to them; that work was honorable, for it was of service to all; and that those who sought to escape their appointed duties and tried, for instance, to make money work for them were anti-social. This is a theory of a static society functionally organized in classes in which there was no room for middlemen. Not that the middlemen who served society and in doing so made an ordinary living were disapproved of; they were recognized, but as commoners performing a necessary function. Only middlemen who tried to profit from their services beyond measure and so disturbed the social and economic equilibrium were deemed as socially unjustified.

In the Renaissance, society had not changed substantially from the medieval pattern. It was still for the most part hierarchically arranged with the old classes at their old tasks. Aristocracy, lay and clerical, still ruled; knights still fought, although they were doing a sorry job at it; and commoners, peasants, craftsmen, and merchants worked to feed and clothe all. Hence there was no call for a new theory of social economy, or even for a modification of the old theory. And so, about the middle of the fifteenth century, Chastellain, the chronicler and poet for the court of Burgundy, still adhered to the old notion. To him, it was by God's decree that commoners tilled the soil and worked at trades, that clergy served at the altar, and that nobility ruled.[15] And because he saw the commoners of his time struggling to reach out beyond their station and knighthood failing in its martial task, he necessarily concluded that these were the reasons for France's sorry state of affairs. A century later Luther was still pursuing the same line. He denounced the demand of the German peasants for the termination of serfdom with the words: "This article would make all men equal. ... Impossible! ... An earthly kingdom cannot exist without inequality of persons. Some must be free, others serfs, some rulers, others subjects."[16] About the same time the English government was requiring that an approved set of sermons be read in the churches. Their theme was the evil of rebellion, which was described as an attempt to violate the order ordained from above. Just as the planetary world was arranged "in a profitable, necessary and pleasant order" so, it was argued, "Every degree of people in the vocation, calling and office, hath appointed to them their duty and order."[17] Thus, until the end of the

Renaissance period, the principle that every class had its calling which had to be fulfilled remained a recognized principle.

Usury[18] The second component of the Renaissance economic theory was the disapproval of usury. Usury in a general sense and from its derivation means the price charged for the use of something. But in the narrow sense and in the sense it was understood by the people of the Middle Ages and the Renaissance it was interpreted as pure interest, that is, a predetermined sum of money that one demanded in return for a loan. This was not limited, as in today's usage, only to cases of excessively high interest charges, but was applied to all interest-taking.

Condemned in the Middle Ages, usury was no less denounced in the days of the Renaissance. From the technical or legalistic point of view, it was considered impossible on the ground that it was a payment for something which did not exist. Money as a thing, it was maintained, and the use of money are not two separate entities, any more than wheat and the use of wheat. The thing and the consumption of the thing in these cases are inseparable; wherefore when one lends money he at the same time lends the use of money, and so there can be no separate charge for its use. Hence pure interest which was claimed to be a charge for the *use* of money was logically impossible.[19] From the social point of view, usury was regarded as a solvent of the existing social order, for it brought forth a class of people who let money work for them and for whom there was no natural place in the ordained social order. Then, from the point of view of religion, it was considered as a surrender to material interests at the risk of man's true end, salvation, and as such it was identified with avarice.

The number of those who took the stand against usury during the Renaissance was legion. In France, for example, there were John Buridan, Nicholas Oresme, and Jean Gerson; in Italy, St. Bernardine of Siena, Alexander Lombard, and St. Antoninus of Florence; in Germany, Cardinal Cajetan; and in Spain, Dominic Soto, councilor and confessor to Emperor Charles V. All were men of great influence in their day, and all preached or wrote against direct usurious transactions, and most of them condemned profit from indirect loans also. Thus Buridan rejected interest-taking on the ground that it was payment for time, something which no man could claim as his own; thus St.

Bernardine and St. Antoninus condemned exchange operations which were not truly exchange transactions; and Soto condemned all exchange deals because he viewed them as subterfuges for loans; thus Alexander Lombard denounced discounting of payments before the due date; and thus St. Antoninus censured guaranteed interest on bank deposits, and even the interest which the borrowers of funds from charitable loan organizations, the *montes,* were expected to pay.

This opposition to usury was not limited to Catholic theologians only: Protestant divines were equally opposed to it. Luther believed that "traffic in interest" was the fundamental cause of the social troubles in Germany and thundered against it from the pulpit and through the press. In his two pamphlets, *Long Sermon on Usury* and *On Trade and Usury,* he decried the recourse to casuistic arguments on the part of its defenders, roundly condemned it as sin, and called for its extirpation. Usury, he insisted, was contrary to Christian charity; wherefore men should help each other in a spirit of brotherhood, advancing loans freely, without any desire for material gain. If man conducted himself thus, then the community of saints would be realized here on earth. For similar reasons Zwingli included usury on a list of sins to be punished by excommunication. So did the ministers of Calvinist Geneva; while Anglican divines deprecated it no end, and Shakespeare, through his Shylock, depicted it as a despicable, anti-social practice.[20]

But widespread as was this condemnation of usury, there were theorists who were prepared to except certain business transactions from the charge of usuriousness. Some of these men date from the Middle Ages, but their number and the number of exceptions they admitted increased during the second half of the Renaissance period.

As an example of a medieval theorist who excepted a transaction from the charge of usury we may point to the great St. Thomas himself. Rationalist that he was, he recognized profit from an investment in partnership (*societas*) as licit, and he based his decision on the premise that the investor who advanced some capital to his partner with which to do business retained the ownership of the money he advanced and ran the risk of loss and was therefore entitled to some profit, if any were forthcoming. As illustrations of the increase in the number of exceptions we may point to the *census* and to the sale of debts. The *census* was a transaction somewhat resembling our annuities. A "buyer" purchased a *census* from a property holder who agreed in return to make a definite number of annual payments to him. In the early Middle Ages the annual payments were actually made in specified commodities raised on the property, but toward the end of the medieval period, the payments were being made in cash, and the transaction really was like a loan repayable in installments and backed by the security of the property in question. And yet this practice was not deemed to be usurious. The same was true of the sale of debt, whether private or public. Thus a person who was obliged to advance money to the state — compulsory loan — could sell the state's promise of repayment for cash, usually at a discount. The purchaser, if he waited until the loan matured, could get the face value of the loan. Hence in buying the debt at the discount, the purchaser was in reality investing money which would bring him what amounted to a guaranteed interest. Yet this practice was not deemed usurious.

During the Renaissance period, especially from the closing decades of the fifteenth century, the attacks on the orthodox views concerning usury became both bolder and broader. How liberal the thinking had become is well illustrated by the positions taken by Conrad Summenhart of the University of Tübingen, by John Eck, the theologian celebrated for his disputation with Martin Luther, and by the French writer Charles Dumoulin.

Summenhart's views appeared in 1499 in his *Treatise on Lawful and Unlawful Contracts*. While he still denounced interest charges on loans to the poor as illicit, he argued, on the other hand, that compensation for loans to businessmen, whether direct or indirect as in partnerships, bills of exchange, and insurance, was not usurious. A loan, he contended, deprived the lender of the use of his money, and the "sacrifice" should be rewarded. At the same time, because a loan brought gain to the borrower, some sharing in the gain was justifiable. But his most sophisticated defense of interest-taking was the argument that money did not have a fixed value, that 100 ducats may be 100 ducats by law, but that the purchasing power of the 100 ducats differed from place to place and from time to time and that any increase in this value should be shared with the lender.

John Eck, though conservative in his theology, was quite liberal in his views on usury. In his *Treatise on the Five Percent Contract* he defended the legality of the contract which combined partnership, loan, and insurance and which provided for 5 per cent profit on the investment. And his defense rested on the argument (1) that, while money may not be productive, industry associated with money made it productive and that the lender who provided the money was entitled to a share of the profit, and (2) that it was not the investor's cupidity which led to the execution of this contract but the borrower's hope of profiting from the loan, wherefore there was no intent to exploit and so no basis for the charge of usuriousness. He also added an argument from practical consideration, namely, that the contract had been in use for so long — some forty years — that it could not be banned without dislocating the business community and bringing hardship on the rest of the people.

Dumoulin's arguments, like Eck's, were based more on the needs of the public than on theoretical principles. The old arguments against usury, he contended in his *Treatise on Contracts and Usury* (1546),[21] were invalid, and irrespective of what the canonists taught and the general public believed, usury was both necessary and indispensable. Without it the wheels of business would falter and the needs of the state could not be met. Moreover, in time of want, it was a source of possible relief even to the poor, for, without the possibility of borrowing, they might be compelled to sell what little property they owned and so deprive themselves of their main hope for security. However, while defending the lawfulness of charging interest, he insisted that the rate was not to exceed any just maximum which the state might prescribe.

Thus by the end of the Renaissance period, while some theorists still denounced usury as sinful and illegal, others — and their number was growing — were justifying it as both licit and socially needful.

JUST PRICE The third element, that of just price, was even more widely advocated than the ban on usury. Usury, as indicated above, applied to the charging of interest for loans. It did not cover other forms of profiteering. Hence another principle had to be devised, one which would apply to the business transactions of craftsmen and merchants. This was the principle of the just price.

By just price the Renaissance man, like his predecessor in the Middle Ages, did not understand some arbitrarily fixed price, but the market price as established by the normal buying and selling operations of all the members of the community. It admitted such determining factors as supply and demand, as well as the costs of production and marketing. But it rejected willful manipulations of the market to increase prices and the deliberate exploitation of the needs of particular individuals. Thus, if a man was desperately in need of bread, he was not to be forced to pay more for it than the normal price: his distress was not to be used to his disadvantage. In sum, just price excluded what we would today call deliberate and outright profiteering.

The grounds for this theory were the same social and moral considerations as stated at the beginning of this section. However, since profiteering in trade jeopardized the welfare of the people more readily and generally than the charging of interest, the moral argument was employed very widely.

As in the case of usury, the theory of just price was constantly reaffirmed throughout the medieval and the Renaissance periods. The same authorities who wrote against usury invariably argued for observance of the principle of just price. Thomas Aquinas treated it in his *Summa Theologica* under the question "On Fraud Committed in Buying and Selling." Three of the subsidiary articles he entitled: "Whether a man may lawfully sell a thing for more than it is worth?" "Whether a sale is rendered unlawful by a defect in a thing sold?" "Whether a seller is bound to declare a defect in a thing sold?" and from the titles themselves it can be gathered that he argued against sharp trading practices. On the other hand, the fourth article he entitled "Whether in trading it is lawful to sell a thing for more than was paid for it?" and therein he pointed out that gain "which is the end of trading, though it does not logically involve anything honorable or necessary, does not logically involve anything sinful or contrary to virtue." But at the same time he added the proviso that gain is not sinful only if it is not contrived by devious manipulations of the market, if it is not sought as an end in itself, and if it is put to proper uses.[22]

A century later, Henry of Langenstein, a university don and a distinguished advocate of conciliarism, included the violators of just price

among those who sought riches "either in order to obtain a higher social position," or to be able to retire, or to raise their sons to "wealth and
importance" and charged them with surrender to "damnable avarice,
sensuality or pride."[23]

Luther thundered for the establishment of a golden age and so denounced attempts at personal enrichment. Trade he admitted as necessary, but he maintained that it was to be motivated by the desire to serve
and that its profits were not to exceed what was needed to compensate
the trader for his labor and risk. The merchant's motto he insisted
should not be "I will sell my wares as dear as I can or please" but "I
will sell my wares as is right and proper."[24] There can be no "smart"
trading.

Calvin, who made a qualified concession as to usury, made no such
concession as to just price. In his opinion men were to "prove themselves Christians by holiness of life," and that hardly admitted of profiteering at the expense of their brethren. And his ministers in Geneva,
taking themselves seriously as guardians of morality in business life
as in other walks of life, constantly sermonized against departures from
this rule and took action through their agency, the Consistory, to enforce it.

Numerous other affirmations of the theory of just price might be
cited. But these few are sufficient, as all that is necessary is to illustrate
the persistence of the theory throughout the Renaissance.

ADHERENCE TO THE THEORY? These three principles constituted the
Renaissance economic theory. The question remains whether the theory
was observed in practice.

We might begin by pointing out that society actually engaged in
the task of securing compliance. The church authorities, both Catholic
and Protestant, tried to enforce the rules: they preached and they prose-
cuted and not infrequently they succeeded in getting the violators to
restitute their ill-gotten gains. State courts were active in the enforce-
ment also. Municipal authorities enacted laws against usury, declared
and enforced price assizes, supervised the weights and measures used
by the merchants, and checked on the quality of goods offered to the
public. Finally, the gilds exercised their general supervisory rights over
their members and tried to prevent fraud in fabrication and to establish

uniform costs and prices. All this agitation against profiteering is an indication of the public's concern about adherence to the theory, and it could not have been wholly in vain: it must have left some impact on those at whom it was aimed, and undoubtedly in many cases it must have prevented deliberate violation by raising moral scruples. This may be surmised from the case of the Spanish speculators on the Antwerp Exchange addressing themselves to the theologians at the University of Paris to find out whether a particular brand of speculation was contrary to canon law, or from such language as the chief bookkeeper of the Fuggers employed when he defined interest-taking as "polite usury" and financing as "polite stealing."[25] And if men like these were wary of ecclesiastical and public opinion, it would not be unreasonable to assume that many lesser merchants and craftsmen were even more respectful of the rules.

On the other hand, the very existence of the well-to-do middle class and of the very rich is obvious evidence that the theory was ignored, for had these "worshipful" people adhered to the rules strictly, they could never have accumulated enough capital to become capitalists. How then can this fact be explained?

Undoubtedly one of the explanations is to be found in the fact that the desire to make money was greater than the inhibitions against it. The fire of the *spiritus capitalisticus,* as the late Professor Pirenne called this desire, was simply too strong to be contained. Its intensity is well reflected in some statements of the contemporaries. Thus Hans Imhof, from Antwerp, wrote to a colleague who had loaned money to the French king: "The investment is safe and the interest good and has helped many a good fellow into the saddle."[26] Giovanni de'Medici, who became head of the Republic of Florence in 1435, is reported to have said: "What I should like would be to have God the Father, God the Son, and God the Holy Ghost, all on my books as debtors."[27] Jacob Fugger, when advised by a relative not to risk his fortune in an especially speculative venture but to safeguard it for the peaceful enjoyment of it in retirement, replied that he "had no intention of doing so," that he "wished to make profit as long as he could."[28] A delightful example comes from the pen of Paolo di Ser Pace da Certaldo, a gildsman of

Florence in the 1300's. In his remarkably frank *Book of Good Examples and Good Manners*, he wrote:

> If thou art engaged in any business and other letters come tied up together with thine own, . . . always remember to read thine own letters before giving the others unto those persons to whom they belong. And if thy letters advise thee to buy or sell any merchandise to thine advantage, send immediately for the broker and do that which thy letters advise, and then afterwards give the letters which came with thine own. But do not give them before thou has concluded thine own business, because those letters could perchance advise something which would injure thy business, and the service which thou has rendered by carrying the letters unto thy *friend or neighbor* [italics added] or unto a stranger might cause great hurt unto thee, and thou shouldst never serve others and thereby hurt thyself or thine own affairs.[29]

Other illustrations could be cited, but these few are sufficient to reveal how strongly the Renaissance men were motivated by the desire to make profit. Such an intense motive could hardly be contained by theories that advocated forbearance, particularly if many of one's associates and competitors were ignoring or circumventing them.

Another explanation is to be found in the fact that the church simply found it impossible to stem the tide and so accommodated itself to it. In the first place, loans to governments and the papacy were exempted from the charge of usury on the ground of their utility. The Venetian budget of 1262, for example, provided for funds to pay the semi-annual 5 per cent interest on the public debt, and the church did not condemn the provision. Loans by kings were not questioned either. Ferñao Lopes, a fourteenth-century chronicler of Portugal, reports that in his day Portuguese kings "lent money on security to all who would borrow and had tithes twice a year for their interest"; while the journal of the banking firm of Pere des Caus and Andreu d'Olivella of Barcelona has an entry giving the amount of interest due from the king and from a duke:

> Due on account of interest to March 31, 1381:
>   (4) on loans to the king . . . . 80,983 11. 11s. 3d.
>   (5) on loans to the Duke of Gerona . . . . 57,913 11. 12s. 6d.[30]

Apparently no religious scruples and no church condemnation were involved in either case. Similarly, profits from land rents were not challenged. In the second place, circumventions were discovered which were of such great utility in the conduct of international business that attempts to ban them would have been impractical and impossible. Some of these, as indicated earlier, were the partnership, insurance, *census,* and the bill of exchange — all of them in part devices for the raising of loans and so for making investments at interest. Thomas Aquinas, it was noted, admitted that the making of profit was not necessarily sinful provided it was not pursued for its own sake but as compensation for the labor expanded on the enterprise. Moreover, he admitted some flexibility when in his explication of the theory he recognized that prices are determined by market potentials as well as by actual costs of materials and labor. He also recognized profits from investment in partnerships as lawful. Then later appeared the rationalizations that justified interest-taking. It will be recalled what Summenhart, Eck, and Dumoulin had to say on this matter. In summary, they and their followers reasoned that a person was entitled to some profit from his loan because he always faced the risk of not being able to recover the loan (*periculum sortis*), or because the repayment might be delayed beyond the term of the loan (*poena conventionalis*), or because by making the loan he denied himself the possibility of making gainful use of his money at the time of the loan (*damnum emergens*) or at some future date (*lucrum cessans*). With these several accommodations available, interest-taking became both legitimate and possible. Finally, and this probably contributed more to the rise of capitalism than some of the preceding factors, neither the church nor society as a whole objected to "conventional practices," and it was business transacted within the limits of "conventional prices" that made many a merchant wealthy. We need only to look around us today to see that "conventional prices" do not militate against the development of big business; and in medieval and Renaissance Florence, it might be pointed out, the "conventional price" for the Calimala merchant included on the average a profit of 12 per cent.

The answer, then, to the question whether the Renaissance society observed the economic theories prevalent in its day, must be, for the most part, in the negative. Men as individuals took cognizance of them and some abided by them; but society as a whole failed to respect them. Man in general was too selfish to abide by the restraints inherent in the theories. On the other hand, the fact that the same society tolerated prosecution for violation of these theories would imply that it still had some scruples on the matter[31] and had not yet arrived at the modern stage of glorifying profit and well-nigh worshiping capital.

Mercantilism

While all the foregoing notions persisted throughout the Renaissance period and constituted Renaissance economic theory, there appeared at the close of the period one additional notion which should be included in this discussion. This was the notion of mercantilism.

In its developed form mercantilism was a theory of planned economy designed to make the state economically sound and politically strong. Some of its isolated roots can be traced back to the first century of the Renaissance, the century of depression, and others even further back to the Middle Ages. Its formulation, however, did not begin until the sixteenth century when the wars between France and Spain (1494–1559), and then between England and Spain (1580's–1604) seriously affected the economies of most of the European countries. And its full development came early in the seventeenth century when Dutch commercial aggressiveness together with the monetary dislocations brought about by the outbreak of the Thirty Years' War (1618–1648) threatened the economic security of western Europe, England in particular, for the second time. During this series of crises, the states found it necessary to regulate their economies ever more widely and, of course, to explain their actions. In time these explanations were fitted together into one comprehensive and related scheme, and this became the celebrated theory of mercantilism.[32]

As a product of national rivalries and economic dislocations, the mercantilist theory naturally concerned itself with the causes of the national weaknesses and with the remedies necessary to overcome them. In its developed form the theory posited that national weakness was due to the scarcity of money, decay of trade and shipping, and to the resulting unemployment; and it insisted that the state had the authority and indeed the duty to plan its economy in such a way as to remedy these conditions.[33]

The heart of the theory was the notion that scarcity of money was the gravest cause of a nation's weakness and that, on the other hand, abundance of money contributed to the nation's strength. To overcome the scarcity of money the theory proposed several obvious measures. On the one hand it advocated full exploitation of native deposits of gold and silver and a determined search for treasure abroad by the discovery of new lands rich in precious minerals. And on the other hand, as means of preserving and augmenting the bullion at home, it urged curtailment of imports of luxury goods, which were normally paid for in money, and the cultivation of a favorable balance of trade. The reasoning behind all this was simple enough: a nation with adequate reserves of precious metal could procure the sinews of war necessary to protect itself and its commerce; and it could promote industry which would produce the finished goods necessary to assure a favorable balance of trade and at the same time provide employment and foster contentment among the laboring classes. In a word, the theory held that possession of money would make for a busy, prosperous, and a happy nation, and so for a strong nation.

To overcome decay of trade and unemployment, the principal remedies suggested were, of course, the acquisition of money and the curtailment of imports, as stated above. But additional methods were also recommended. One recommendation was that colonies be founded and their markets monopolized; another, that new industries be established and those in decay stimulated; and still another, that public works be undertaken, such as the building of port installations, which in turn would facilitate trade. While each of these remedies individually was deemed capable of reducing unemployment and increasing trade, truly great benefits were expected from their cumulative effects.

Next to the availability of treasure, the theory insisted on adequate shipping as the second most important means for the promotion of the nation's welfare. Everything depended upon the nation's ability to preserve its security, to defend its trade routes, and to protect its old markets and to secure new ones. Hence the nation was obliged to create an effective merchant marine and a strong navy. It could do so by enacting navigation laws in favor of national shipping, by expanding shipyards and port facilities, by encouraging the fishing industry, the training school for seamen, and by securing a safe source of materials for shipbuilding.

Another point which the theory included was the full utilization of available manpower. As was pointed out above, most countries during the Renaissance were plagued with unemployment, idleness, and vagrancy. These conditions not only invited social disorder, but they also were a drain on the nation's economy. It was natural therefore for a theory which undertook to prescribe remedies for strengthening the nation to include this problem within its purview. It did so in connection with all the major recommendations already mentioned. Increased manufacturing, expansion of shipping and of the navy, founding of colonies — all were justified on the ground that they would help to relieve unemployment. However, it also provided a separate recommendation. It advocated public works, compulsory labor for the idle who were physically fit, and public support for the incapacitated. This would contribute to the elimination of idleness and vagrancy and add to the improvement of public utilities. In a word, a public works program would contribute to the stability and the strength of the nation.

Such in essence was the theory of mercantilism. What it amounted to was an explanation of a nation's economic ills and a series of recommendations to remedy same. Most proposals envisaged state action designed to keep the nation prosperous and strong. Since the states were doing just this in ever-increasing degree, the theory may well be regarded as a comprehensive rationalization of state-planned economy already substantially under way. The theory was not born *ab ovo,* and it did not inaugurate a new economic program. All it did was to provide philosophical sanction for what was already in the making.

1. For a detailed treatment of the subject through the fifteenth century see *CEcH,* III, 290–419.
2. Thomas N. Bisson, "Coinages and Royal Monetary Policy in Languedoc during the Reign of St. Louis," *Speculum,* XXXII (1957), 443–69.
3. For an excellent study of this experimentation see Frederic C. Lane, "Venetian Merchant Galleys, 1300–1334," *Speculum,* XXXVIII (1963), 179–203.
4. Klein, *op. cit.,* 49.

5. Diffie, *op. cit., passim*, and James Westfall Thompson, *An Economic and Social History of the Middle Ages, 300–1300* (New York: The Century Co., 1926), 476, 477, 480, 482, 486, 493, 496.

6. *CEcH*, I, 335–6.

7. See E. B. Fryde, "Financial Resources of Edward I in the Netherlands, 1294–98: Main Problems and Some Comparisons with Edward IV in 1337–40," *RB*, XL (1962), 1168–87.

8. *CEcH*, I, 356.

9. On the staples see Edwin Ernest Rich, *The Ordinance Book of the Merchants of the Staple* (Cambridge: The University Press, 1937); Eileen Power, *The Wool Trade in English Medieval History*, 86–103; *CEcH*, III, 352–3.

10. A. E. Bland, P. A. Brown, R. H. Tawney, *English Economic History, Select Documents* (London: G. Bell and Sons, Ltd., 1914), 314; R. Vivier, "Crise économique au milieu du xivᵉ siècle; la première intervention de la royauté dans le domaine économique," *Revue d'histoire économique et sociale*, VIII (1920), 199–230.

11. For an account of one of these poor laws antedating the celebrated law enacted in Elizabeth's reign see G. R. Elton, "An Early Tudor Poor Law," *EcHR*, 2d series, VI (1953), 55–67.

12. An introductory but a highly suggestive treatment of this subject is to be found in Jean Hippolyte Mariéjols *The Spain of Ferdinand and Isabella*, trans. Benjamin Keen (New Brunswick, New Jersey: Rutgers University Press, 1961), 209–22.

13. Eli F. Heckscher, *Mercantilism*, trans. M. Shapiro and rev. E. F. Söderlund (New York: The Macmillan Co., 1955), I, 50.

14. William Harrison, *A Description of Britain and England*, vol. XXXV of *Harvard Classics* (New York: P. F. Collier and Son, 1910), 261.

15. Johan Huizinga, *The Waning of the Middle Ages* (Garden City, New York: Doubleday and Company, Inc., 1954), 59–60.

16. Cited from R. H. Tawney, *Religion and the Rise of Capitalism* (Baltimore: Penguin Books Limited, 1938), 96.

17. Cited from Christopher Morris, *Political Thought in England, Tyndale to Hooker* (London: Oxford University Press, 1953), 74.

18. The best treatment of the subject in English language is John T. Noonan, Jr., *The Scholastic Analysis of Usury* (Cambridge: Harvard University Press, 1957). This is a study of the theories from 1150 to 1750.

19. The argument is from Thomas Aquinas' *Summa Theologeia* and may be read in translation in Arthur Eli Monroe's *Early Economic Thought* (Cambridge: Harvard University Press, 1924), 65–69.

20. Shakespeare's attitude to usury is discussed in E. C. Pettet, "The Merchant of Venice and the Problem of Usury," *Essays and Studies by Members of the English Association,* XXXI (1945), 19–33.

21. Long excerpt in translation is to be found in Monroe, *op. cit.,* 105–20.

22. *Ibid.,* 63–64.

23. Tawney, *Religion and the Rise of Capitalism,* 48.

24. *Ibid.,* 95–97.

25. Mildred L. Hartsough, *op. cit.,* 545.

26. Cited from Ehrenberg, *op. cit.,* 305.

27. F. Funck-Bretano, *The Renaissance* (New York: The Macmillan Co., 1936), 45.

28. Strieder, *op. cit.,* 12.

29. Cited from Guido Biagi, *Men and Manners of Old Florence* (London: T. Fisher Unwin, 1909), 79–80.

30. Cf. Livermore, *op. cit.,* 164, and Usher, *op. cit.,* 260. For examples of interest-bearing state loans in Italian cities see Luzzatto, *op. cit.,* 121–6.

31. Apropos this matter of conscience versus profit in the late Renaissance see Renee Doehaerd, "Commerce et morale à Anvers au xvie siècle," *Revue historique,* CCIV (1950), 226–33.

32. The classic exposition remains Heckscher's *Mercantilism.* For a brief citicism of his thesis see Edmund Whittaker, *A History of Economic Ideas* (New York: Longman's Green and Co., 1950), 93–95. On the genesis of the theory there are valuable remarks in R. W. K. Hinton's "The Mercantile System in the Time of Thomas Mun," *EcHR,* 2d series, VII (1955), 277–90, and J. D. Gould's "The Trade Depression of the Early 1620's," 81–90, of the same journal and issue.

33. For succinct statements on these points by some Renaissance political economists see Charles Woolsey Cole, *French Mercantilist Doctrines before Colbert* (New York: Richard R. Smith, Inc., 1931).

CHAPTER VI ~ *Renaissance Society*

I NTRODUCTION Renaissance society, if it is to be depicted truly, must be depicted completely. The description should not concentrate only on the more brilliant aspects of society, on the glitter of the aristocracy and on the enterprise of the moneyed class, as is sometimes done;[1] it should also include the vast darksome background represented by the masses. Some three quarters of the population cannot be omitted from the canvass and still leave the picture true to reality.

People of the "Meanest" Class

In the days of the Renaissance this class, called *vilissimi* and presumed to be lacking in the blood necessary for high virtues and duties, was comprised of the peasantry and of the urban proletariat, though the term was more generally applied to the former than to the latter. The peasant class consisted of serfs (still numerous in central and eastern France and east of the Elbe), of tenants, landless farm laborers, and the poor landed proprietors; and throughout Europe this class constituted the great majority of the population. The urban proletariat was made up of the poorer craftsmen, apprentices, day laborers, street-hawkers, boatmen, servants, and vagabonds. In the towns this class also constituted the great majority. Combined, the peasants and the town masses probably made up more than 75 per cent of the entire population. In the interest of historical truth and perspective the way of life of this vast majority demands due consideration.

PEASANTRY — CONDITION OF LIFE The condition of peasant life varied from place to place and from time to time. It depended on such variables as fertility of lands, type of farming, density of local population, market possibilities, and political climate. Obviously it would be impossible to give a generalized picture which would hold true for all Europe and for the entire Renaissance period. To every such picture so many exceptions could be raised as to invalidate it. Still, some attempt at a general delineation needs to be made.

121

We might begin by pointing out that throughout the entire period and in all the lands the great majority of the peasants were not yet owners of their own farms but tenants. They either share-cropped or paid a specified amount of rent in kind and cash. Except for variations in the less important aspects of the lease, share-cropping was on a one-to-one or on a two-to-one basis, two parts of the returns from the farm for the owner and one part for the peasant. The terms of the lease varied, but the value of the rent approximated the value of the returns from share-cropping. Another fact which was quite general was the small size of the farms the peasants operated. Grain farms of ten acres or more and vineyards of two or three acres were regarded as substantial farms, most were smaller. Still another general fact was the low yield of the arable, five to six times the amount of seed put in, or ten to twelve bushels per acre. Finally, most peasants farmed in accordance with the two- or three-year system of crop rotation, and this meant that only one half or two-thirds of their arable was in crop.

Taking all these things into consideration we cannot escape the conclusion that the peasant's income from the arable was small and that his lot was a hard one. To be sure most peasants raised some cattle, pigs, and poultry, thereby supplementing their food supplies and adding a few pennies now and then to their purses. Many also secured seasonal work on the larger estates or, if they lived in cloth-manufacturing areas, took in some wool to spin and weave at piece-work rates. But these supplementary sources of income did not yield much. Stock raising, for instance, could not be conducted on a large scale by individual peasants because they were unable to raise sufficient fodder for winter; and piece-work rates were low, lower than in towns, and these were low enough. While some relief was forthcoming from these sources, it was not enough to alter the living standards substantially. The mass of the peasants simply led a life which was barely above subsistence level.

This indigence appears to have been widespread and was a frequent topic for comment in all the lands of Europe during most of the Renaissance period.

In France, where the ravages of the Hundred Years' War aggravated this poverty, the picture is truly pitiful. Here is what Gerson, Chancellor of the University of Paris, said about the condition of his peasant countrymen when he preached a court sermon in November, 1405:

> The poor man will not have bread to eat, except perhaps a handful of rye and barley; his poor wife will lie in and they will have four to six little ones about the hearth of the oven, which perchance will be warm; they will ask for bread, they will scream mad with hunger. The poor mother will but have very little salted bread to put to their mouths.[2]

Sir John Fortescue's description, now something of a classic, is no more comforting even if we take into account his implied moral that the third estate, because of its impotence, was itself responsible for the misery it had to bear:

> . . . the same commons be so impoverysshid and distroyed, that thai nowe vnneth leve, thai drinken water, thai eyten apples, with brede right browne made of rye; thai eyten no flesshe but yf it be right seldon a little larde, or of the entrales and heydes of bestis slayn for the nobles and marchauntes of the lands. Thai weren no wolen, but yf it be a pouere cote vundir thair vttermost garnement, made of grete caunuas, and callid a frokke. Thair hausyn beth of lyke caunuas, and passyn not thair kne, wherefore thai beth gartered and ther theis bare. Thair wyfes and childeren gone bare fote; thai mowe in non other wyse leve. . . . Wher thurgh thai be arted bi necessite so to wacch, labour, and grubbe in the ground for thair sustenance, that thair nature is wasted, and the kynde of hem broght to noght. Thai gon crokyd, and ben feble, not able to fight, nor to defende the realme; nor thai have wepen, nor money to bei thaim wepen with all. But verely thai liven in the most extreme pouertie and miserie. . . .[3]

Equally intolerable were the conditions reported to the Estates General of 1484. According to the reports of some deputies the countryside was full of misery and suffering, with mothers and children, half-naked, wandering off into the woods and mountains in search of herbs and roots and dying of hunger, and with despondent fathers even doing away with their families.[4] No doubt these accounts were exaggerated, as the representatives who painted these bleak pictures were arguing for lower tax assessments against their districts. Still, the picture of widespread poverty and starvation was basically true. If after a while conditions brightened, it was not for long; for within several decades the peasant's lot, overwhelmed by the price revolution and by the prolonged

and bitter Wars of Religion, became deplorable once more. The stark
picture by the poet Pierre du Laval of the sacking of the peasants' homesteads depicts a truly hopeless prospect

> . . . one saw his barns empty
> And his house bereft of furniture and other belongings:
> Not even a cot was left him, nothing at all.[5]

In England there was no Hundred Years' War to ravage and to
waste the countryside. Nevertheless the peasant's poverty was widespread. In the fourteenth century, Langland's realistic picture is that of
a humble and indigent peasantry:

> "I've no penny," quoth Piers, "young pullets to buy
> Nor bacon nor geese, only two green cheeses
> Some curds and some cream, and an oaten cake,
> Two bean-loaves with bran, just baked for my children
> And I say, by my soul, I have no salt bacon,
> Nor eggs, by my Christendom, collops to make;
> Only onions and parsley, and cabbage-like plants;
> Eke a cow and a calf, and an old cart-mare
> To draw afield dung, while the drought shall prevail."[6]

John Ball's picture is bitter, and, as a would-be social leveler, he com-
plains of peasantry that had "only rye [to eat] and the refuse of the
straw; and if [they] did drink it must be water."[7] In the following
century Thomas More in his protest against enclosures saw the unfortunate peasants as "poor silly wretched souls" with large families, and
households "small in substance [and] very little worth."[8]

These pictures of poverty among French and English peasantry are
duplicated in Germany. The account of Hans Beham is like an echo
of Langland:

> The fourth and last class of Germans are those who live on the land
> in villages and hamlets and who till the land, wherefore they are called
> rustics or countryfolk. If they will believe it, their condition is very
> wretched and hard. They live apart from the rest, in lowly fashion,
> each with his household and his beasts. Their cottages are of mud
> and timber, rising little above the ground, and covered with straw.
> They feed on brown bread, oatmeal porridge, or boiled peas; they
> drink water or whey; they are clad in linen coat, with boots of un-
> tanned leather and a dyed cap. They are ever an unquiet crew, la-
> borious and unclean.[9]

In Brabant and Hainaut, toward the end of the fifteenth century (1496), there were country regions where approximately 50 per cent of the householders were too poor to be taxed, and thirty years later the situation was still almost as bad even though the war ravages of the earlier period had been healed.[10]

In Italy, where the recurrent interurban wars plagued the defenseless countryside, the plight of the peasantry was no brighter. Luca Landucci, a Florentine apothecary who has left a revealing diary of affairs in Florence after 1450, seldom speaks of these people without referring to their destitution:

> It was a most pitiful sight to see these poor people pass, with a wretched little donkey, and their miserable household possessions; saucepans, frying pans, etc. One wept to see them barefoot and ragged; . . .
> And we heard that a poor peasant, who had come to Florence to beg for bread, having left three small children starving at home, finding them dying on his return, and not being able to succour them, took a rope and hung himself.
> The poor women and children (of the plain of Prato) were laden with their scanty possessions; anyone who saw them could not help feeling moved and forced to weep.[11]

Such was the lot of many peasants throughout Europe. But this somber picture while widespread was not universal. There was a great number of peasants, and a growing number of them, who, for one reason or another, were able to improve their lot.

Among the more fortunate peasants were those who operated their own farms and lived close enough to a large city to profit from its demands for farm products. In Middlesex, for example, in Elizabeth's day, as reported by Norden in his *Mirror of Britain,* the farms were

> . . . so furnished with kine that the wife twice or thrice a week conveyeth to London milk, butter, cheese, apples, pears, frumenty, hens, chickens, eggs, bacon and a thousand other country drugs, which good housewives can frame and find to get a penny. And this yielded them a large comfort and relief.[12]

Those who possessed surpluses to sell profited also from price rises. Thus in Burgundy, according to the caustic remarks of Alain Chartier,

... the common folk have this advantage that their purses are like a cistern which has gathered and continues to gather water and drops from all the riches of the kingdom. The rise in prices has reduced the value of their rents and services and their outrageous charges for food stocks and labour daily increase their wealth.[13]

Similar reports of prosperity come from other lands also. In Germany, in the words of Jacob Wimpfeling, one of the leaders of the Renaissance there:

The prosperity of the peasants here (Alsace) and in most parts of Germany has made them proud and luxurious. I know peasants who spend as much at the marriage of their sons and daughters or the baptism of their infants as would buy a small house and farm or vineyard. They are extravagant in their dress and living, and drink costly wines.[14]

An Austrian chronicler once reported that the Austrian peasants "wear better garments and drink better wines than their lords." Another claimed that the peasants were rich and wore fine clothes "as nobility and citizens in easy circumstances wore in former times"; and still another reported of a Westphalian noble who complained that the credit of a peasant was greater than that of ten nobles.[15]

Although some of these reports are clearly farfetched, there is a residue of truth in them. They must be accepted as evidence of the existence of prosperous peasantry.[16] Hence the total picture is a dual one — it reveals a minority which enjoyed relative prosperity and a majority which had a hard life.

For those with meager resources, and sometimes for the others also, the lot became unbearable when the normal state of affairs was disturbed. A crop failure or two, an increase in state exactions and in rent, or devastation from war would reduce them to destitution. Sometimes this taxed their endurance, and then under some irritation, real or fancied, they rose in rebellion and threatened to overthrow the existing social and economic system. Such was the Jacquerie in France in 1358; such in part was the Hussite Revolt, which mixed religious reform and national reaction with proletarian communism; such were the frequent peasants' revolts in Germany — in 1432, 1437, 1476, 1491, 1502, 1513 — and the Great Peasants' Revolt in 1524–25; and such was Kett's rebellion in England in 1549. But not one of these revolts succeeded; after their initial outburst, the peasants were checked, slaughtered like helpless sheep, and driven back to their lands to eke out a miserable living from the niggardly soil.

However, lest we get the picture that the peasant's life was one long, drawn-out day of woe, we should keep in mind that if he was poor, his poverty, unless aggravated beyond the customary, did not rest too heavily on his mind and did not prevent him from finding satisfaction in life. A Venetian ambassador entering France from Spain in 1528 was impressed by the geniality of the populace in Bayonne.[17] Beham's statement "if they will believe it, their condition is very wretched and hard" clearly suggests that their poverty did not perpetually prey on their minds. Again, the *genre* pictures of peasantry by the Elder Brueghel, in particular the "Peasants' Dance," "The Wedding Dance," and "The Wheat Harvest," may be taken as authentic evidence of the lighter side of peasant life.

In addition to his farm, the peasant possessed a few appurtenances and some stock. A cow, possibly an ox or two or even a horse, a hog or two or sometimes a whole litter, a few sheep and a small flock of fowl comprised his stock. To shelter these he had a barn, which frequently was but another room attached to his house; and to preserve fodder for them he probably had a corn rick. Of farm implements and of other instruments of labor he had a plow and a cart, a number of hoes, sickles, scythes, rakes and flails, some axes and a few carpenters' tools. Of course, there was the inevitable spinning wheel.

His house generally was a one-room mud hut with a thatched roof and a mud floor. It usually was without a chimney, and its windows were ordinarily covered with greased cloth or skins instead of glass. In it there was a hearth of clay in which he burned fallen branches, peat, or even dry manure. His furniture consisted of a crude bed — or he slept on a pile of straw in one corner of the room — a rough-hewn table, a chest or two where he kept his linens and Sunday clothes and his small hard-earned savings, a long bench, a wooden churn and buckets, and a suspended crossbar upon which to hang his work clothes or his smoked bacon or sausage if he had any.[18]

His dress, though subject to changes in style, was made at home or by an itinerant craftsman, coarse and heavy but durable, often untidy from long wear.[19] Womenfolk possessed a change or two, and their festive clothes were as picturesque in design as they were rich in color. Only an inordinately foolish peasant would sell "a cow against Easter to buy him silken gear."[20]

His food was very simple fare — rye bread and oaten or barley biscuit, salted and washed down with water, whey, cider, or beer, often in generous quantities; herrings and saltdry fish on lenten days, salt pork and old cheese on other days; some vegetables, onion, garlic, cabbage, peas and beans, but no potatoes; some fruit in season where available; beef only when it was necessary to kill an animal for lack of fodder or from age or injury; perhaps some pork, mutton, or fowl on festive days.[21]

As a villager the peasant had little acquaintance with the world. Some national and regional news he probably picked up at a mission held by some mendicant friar, or at a local fair, or possibly at an inn where, unbeknown to his wife, he may have slipped in for a beer. Of local gossip he knew plenty, but of world events, such as the discoveries of the new worlds, he heard little and understood less. Just as most people of today pay little heed to the fact that they live in an atomic age, so most people then were unaware that they were living in an age of new discoveries, geographic and scientific.

Born and raised as a child of the soil, the peasant was illiterate. He probably was capable of some mental reckoning, but it was only the lucky son who may have found his way into church or into some business in town and there secured formal schooling. But what the peasant lacked in letters he made up in familiarity, by rote, with church services and long prayers. If he became a Protestant, he listened to the gospel but he knew little about the theological issues involved. In general, he was conservative and disliked innovations which disturbed his spiritual equanimity. He was profoundly superstitious, and he knew the hidden meaning behind every last phenomenon. His language was coarse and vulgar; and, in keeping with his rough tongue, his person was unkempt and his manners boorish. Everywhere he was looked down upon as an object of derision, a person at whom one is tempted to laugh and with whom one is likely to commiserate. Thomas Churchyard's characterization of him in *The Spider and the Gout* seems best to capture that mixture of sentiments:

> This grunting grub was short and thick,
> His face was red as any brick,
> Wherein there stood a bottle-nose;
> A couple of corns upon his toes
> He had, which made him cut his shoe;
> He never put on garments new
> But when that to the wakes he went,
> He was dressed up like Jack a Lent.[22]

Compared with the conditions of peasant life in the twelfth and thirteenth centuries there is very little difference.[23] The peasant of the Renaissance probably bought a few more things. If he were one of the more fortunate ones, he probably had a house of timber or stone, with glass windows and a chimney, and some used furniture.[24] But for the most part his material conditions remained as they were before. It is true that an increasing number of the peasantry were gaining freedom and that in wide sections of Europe serfdom actually disappeared, but for most of the liberated peasantry this boon was a gain more in law and in social standing than in material welfare. In fact, during the Renaissance he was losing in security what he may have been gaining in status.[25] Hence poor and ignorant and despised, the peasant provides the dark background which shadows the glory of the Renaissance. In the majority of cases, as far as the peasant's standard of living was concerned, the Renaissance was a period of continuity; perhaps, as was true of the peasantry from the Elbe and the Danube to the Vistula, it actually turned out to be a period of retrogression;[26] and he constituted the bulk of the population in western Europe.

Town Proletariat Just as the majority of the country folk belonged to the "meanest" class of people, so did the greater portion of the urban inhabitants. Whether a small craftsman, journeyman, or apprentice; whether a servant, or vagabond; whether a hawker or a boatman, this town resident invariably was looked down upon as a member of the lowest class in society. Sometimes his very skill was turned against him as a mark of contempt and opprobrium. Thus, in Flanders, all those connected with the dyeing industry were contemptuously referred to as the "blue nails." In Florence the poorer artisans were called the "Ciompi," that is, "bare feet," from the fact that many of the poorer people belonged to the gild of the fullers who "fulled" their cloth by stamping over it with their bare feet in a tank of fuller's brine.

Regarded as socially inferior, and in many places treated by the higher classes as politically rightless,[27] this proletariat led a miserable life. Their income, whether derived from business or from wages, was incredibly low and often insufficient for the barest necessities. In many English country towns, for example, in the 1520's, on the basis of subsidy returns for 1524–1525, between one-fourth and one half of the residents possessed property or annual income which could not be assessed at £2, and as many again who just made the £2 assessment.[28] Even though these assessments were naturally below the real value of the property or the income assessed, there can be no doubt that they represent wordly possessions which were hardly enough even for the most frugal subsistence. Of course, when unemployment hit or when inflation ate away even these meager earnings, these unfortunates could not procure event the barest necessities, and so many became public charges. In some Belgium towns, for example, the number of the urban poor on relief doubled or tripled in the ninety years between 1437 and 1526. Thus in Louvain it rose from 7.6 per cent of the population to 21.7 per cent, and in Brussels from 10.5 per cent to 21 per cent.[29] And when this poverty became unbearable, it provoked strikes and uprisings. The journeymen tailors in Wessel, for example, struck in 1503 because, in the words of the mayor who tried to settle the dispute, "the masters overpower[ed] them with work and [did] not give them three good meals a day."[30] But perhaps the most galling fact was not the inadequacy of their incomes, but the gnawing awareness on their part of the tremendous economic disparity between the rich merchant class and themselves. Poverty becomes oppressive when contrasted with wealth.

Their barest necessities in the way of housing, diet, and clothing were not much better than those of the peasants in the country. For homes they had one- or two-chambered buildings of wood or of wood and clay, or they crowded their families into single rooms in old and crowded alley tenements. Some of them, specifically the apprentices and servants, lived with their masters, but even so, the quarters set aside for them were usually quite mean. In these homes the furnishings were notable either for their crudity or for their absence. Chimneys were more common than in the homes of the peasants, as were possibly glass windows and some pewter ware. As to clothing there was little difference in quantity or quality, except perhaps for shoes, the peasantry often going about their business unshod. But if some members of the proletariat class had more adequate living quarters and clothing, they did not have a more adequate diet. Thus, according to Villon's account in the *Great Testament,* cxxxiii, the poor Parisian's food consisted of "bread . . . garnished . . . with onions fit to force the face away . . . , cheese . . . curds . . . whey . . . barley bread or oat, not made with yeast, washed down with water all year round."[31] They may even have had a less certain supply of food. For while some were fortunate enough to have gardens attached to their houses and thus were able to grow a few vegetables, all had to procure their bread and oatmeal and salt and fish on the market; and as the price of the foodstuffs was increasing more rapidly than their wages, their larder, like that of the proverbial Mother Hubbard, was frequently bare. On the other hand, exposed to greater temptations, some of the townsmen yielded to improvidence and tried to live beyond their means, in which case the price of indulgence one day was real want the next day. And when this happened, one either turned to thievery, or to begging, or to one of the many almshouses that dotted the cities, or to the patronage of some wealthy man. It is reported, for example, that Thomas Cromwell, chancellor of England's Henry VIII, fed some 200 poor daily at the gate of his London residence.

Like the peasantry, the majority of the proletariat was illiterate. But it probably was more worldly-wise. The inns, the markets, the shipping docks were all replete with news, both national and international; and these the townsmen, poor as well as rich, followed with enthusiasm, though perhaps without much understanding except where the information adversely affected their own material welfare. Then they would complain and demand protective measures, or even riot.

Comparing the lot of the urban low class in the Renaissance with the conditions of the same group in the pre-Renaissance period, one cannot find a significant improvement. Even if more homes were now tiled

instead of thatched, even if the food and clothing markets offered more
and a greater variety of things for sale, the poor townsman found himself behind in the race against rising prices, and his standard of living
necessarily suffered. In desperation he turned to vagabondage, and his
wife and children became waifs of the streets.[32] It is no wonder therefore that Renaissance Europe had more beggars than any other age,
and that states began to enact poor laws.

The Middle Class

COMPOSITION AND PROMINENCE OF THE CLASS Above the "meanest"
folk stood the *bons gens*, the *goede lieden*, the "decent people" of the
middle class. This class was comprised of several elements. The most
important group was that of the substantial tradesmen and craftsmen,
the true burgesses, distinguished by such designations as the "more
sufficient," the "worshipful," and "the discreet." Next came the group
made up of professional people, particularly those trained in law, and
those holding administrative offices, local or national.

Beginning in the tenth century, the class grew through the years
as the revival of commerce and industry increased its numbers and the
wealth of its members. It organized itself into various gilds, secured
the incorporation of towns, and then monopolized the town governments. In time these gains won it a place in state governments. In England and Spain it obtained a definite place in the chief governing
bodies, the parliament and the cortes respectively, by the end of the
thirteenth century. In France, as the Third Estate, it began to be consulted by Philip IV when he clashed with Pope Boniface VIII in the
1290's. And in the 1350's when John the Good and the nobility had
demonstrated their incapacity to serve the nation by losing the battles
of Crecy and Poitiers to the English, the bourgeois of Paris actually
tried to establish themselves as the preponderant partner in the government of the land. In northern and central Italy, in most of the larger
towns, it actually succeeded in establishing itself through a variety of
republican constitutions as the sole political authority.[33]

Solidly established by the middle of the fourteenth century, this middle class maintained its position during the Renaissance. Here and
there it yielded political leadership to the princely merchant class, as in

Florence to the Medici and in Augsburg to the Fuggers, but in provincial towns, such as Toulouse, where there was less opportunity for international finance, it preserved its position and influence unchallenged.[34]

GENERAL BOURGEOIS TRAITS The class in general was possessed of several bourgeois traits. One of these was the spirit of enterprise. Its members strove to increase their wealth, to get into government posts, and to win social prestige; and they liked to display their hard-earned success. Another trait was practical-mindedness. Since education was one road to success for them, they sent their sons to schools, they promoted municipal schooling and tried to wrest control of education from the church authorities. They read books on proper conduct with the view of "getting on" in the world. Another typical bourgeois trait was the concern for order. They were proponents of social tranquility, of the rule of law, and of the sanctity of property, all of which were obviously good for business. They were civic minded, and sought to protect the interests of their town, which incidentally they identified with their own. In sum, they showed themselves as dynamic and confident and substantial. After all, did they not refer to themselves as the "more sufficient" and "discreet"?

STANDARD OF LIVING In the period of the Renaissance this middle class had a substantial standard of living. Their homes, storied and steep-gabled and crowded together along the narrow streets, were generally built of timber and plaster and as yet only occasionally of stone or brick. Compact in appearance, with the ground floor used as a shop, the basement as a warehouse, and the upper stories as living quarters for servants and proprietors, the homes were nevertheless serviceable and comfortably furnished. The furnishings, substantial in appearance, consisted of various tables, benches, chairs, chests, stools, washbasins (sometimes silver), clothes presses, canopied beds, cushions, featherbeds, patterned coverlets, canvas-lined draperies, colorful tapestries, and sometimes rugs and skins. Their trestle tables, or the newly appearing tables "dormant," were laden not only with ample food, particularly meats of several varieties, sauces, pastries, ales and wines, but also with pewter and with some silverware. They had adequate clothing, several changes at least, black and russet cloth for everyday wear, and, for festive occasions, silk and velvet, which, if not quite foppish, were certainly trim and in style. Sometimes their tastes got beyond their sober judgment and they put on finery reserved for the nobility alone, cloth of gold and silver and furs,[35] but they were promptly reminded by repeated enactments of sumptuary laws of having overreached their proper ranks. In general, one gets the impression that this class was earnest, and solid, and comfortable. For all these particulars the reader would do well to consult the excellent description of the three men of this class that Professor Eileen Power provides in her charming book, *Medieval People.* The first of these, the Menagier de Paris, is an elderly man of sixty years plus, well-to-do, and husband of a very young wife who just turned sixteen. For her instruction and benefit he composed a little treatise on how to make a dutiful and affectionate wife, an expert housekeeper, and a charming hostess. The other two figures are Thomas Betson, an English wool exporter of the second half of the fifteenth century, and Thomas Paycocke of Coggeshall, an Essex clothier in the days of Henry VII of England. From Professor Power's perceptive account of these men, it is quite easy to discern the energetic spirit and the solid substance of this class.

LIFE OF A GENOESE BUSINESSMAN AS AN EXAMPLE To select some one family as typical of the class is, of course, impossible. Nevertheless, a look at the life of one of its members is decidedly worthwhile, as it may impart some realism to the generalized picture presented above. Professor Power treats of a Frenchman and two Englishmen; let us look at an Italian, Giovanni Piccamiglio, a prominent Genoese businessman.[36]

In the era of the crusades, when Genoa's economy was booming and its merchants waxing rich, Giovanni's ancestors were among the topmost families, perhaps even of noble status, as Genoese social standards sanctioned the participation of nobility in business activities. By the fifteenth century, however, the family had dropped from its earlier high estate to the level of a prosperous bourgeois, although by marriage to the Fieschi, one of the very highest families in the city, Giovanni was still tied to the aristocracy and was himself rated high enough to hold important civic offices — in 1454 and 1461 as a member of the Council of Ancients, in 1460 among the "Padri del Commune," and in 1458 and 1469 as director of the state bank, the Bank of St. George.

Giovanni started his career as a merchant dealing in goods of the Near East. In 1445, for example, he was in Chios gathering a cargo for the west, alum especially; and in 1450, he spent six months in Pera, the famous Genoese outpost on the Bosporus. Subsequently, he stayed in Genoa, managing several pieces of business property, which he inherited, and doing business as a merchant, broker, and banker under the name Giovanni Piccamiglio and Company; and it was during this time that he compiled his famous register — still in Latin incidentally — covering his business transactions from January, 1456, through most of July, 1459, which provides some information on his habits of life as well as on his business activities.

Although he had given up adventuring, Giovanni still engaged in merchandising, but mainly as a contributor of capital and only as a secondary interest, since his investment in these ventures by 1459 amounted to only 1,940 *lire* and his profit to 145 *lire*. He was more active as a marine insurance broker. But here, too, fortune did not smile on him, for on a sale of thirty-nine policies valued at 6,607 *lire,* his profit in this three-year period amounted to only 42 *lire.* He had better luck with his loan business. On one loan of 405 *lire* for thirty-eight months he charged 195 *lire* as interest, and on another of 2,000 *lire* he netted 14.8 per cent annually. Even more profitable was his speculation in stocks of the Bank of St. George and of other concerns. On one occasion, on an investment of $1,262\frac{1}{2}$ *lire* for fifty shares of the Bank — really state bonds — he made in thirteen months, $261\frac{1}{2}$ *lire*. On another occasion his profit amounted to 32.5 per cent in a two-month period. Several other purchases were only a little less profitable. Finally, he dealt in letters of exchange: in the three-year period of the journal the total capital involved in this business amounted to 159,710 *lire* — and his profit was 2,685 *lire*.

Piccamiglio's living standard was commensurate with his income, although on occasion, when status demanded, he seems to have yielded to some extravagance. His townhouse where he lived with his wife, three daughters, two sons, and three slaves (two as nurses for his daughters and a messenger boy) was assessed at 216 *lire,* obviously not a pretentious structure; and he bought a country home with a vineyard and some arable for 615 *lire*. We do not know how expensively his homes were furnished, but he kept a record of his food bills. His provisions, much of which he imported, consisted of solid staples, wheat, bread, wine — only a small portion of which was of the exotic variety — fish, meat, sugar, spices, and some caviar, and cost about 150 *lire* per year. His taste for clothing was more extravagant, as he purchased items of fur, velours, and of other luxury cloths; but it was not beyond him to use "scab" labor to put the garments together. Like most fathers who want to make an impression when they give their daughters in marriage, Giovanni really splurged when he married off one of his daughters — he gave her a dowry of 3,000 *lire,* bought her a home valued at 582 *lire,* and spent on the trousseau and reception almost three times the value of his own town home, a total of 678 *lire*.

All this points to a comfortable and substantial life, proper for a solid businessman who held important civic offices and who, while not of the aristocratic class, was not far below it.

Gentry

ORIGIN AND GROWTH By gentry we mean the non-noble class of gentlemen landlords who possessed good-sized farms which they either operated themselves or leased out to tenants. The class appeared in the late Middle Ages and thereafter grew to such proportions that it became a significant social force in the Renaissance period.[37]

The class recruited itself from several sources. Some of its members were descendants of enterprising peasants who, after their liberation from serfdom, became tenants and later owners of lands which they kept enlarging until the income from these holdings enabled them to live as gentlemen farmers. Usually, it took several generations before the peasant stigma wore off sufficiently to enable these people to gain acceptance as gentlefolk, but some made the grade, and their numbers increased steadily in the course of the Renaissance period. Many members of the class were merchants or civil servants, some who purchased income-bearing estates with the view of retiring to them, and others who acquired them as an investment and combined farming with their former vocations. Some members were descendants of former knightly families who found themselves increasingly confined to farming as their feudal functions diminished with the rise of effective monarchic governments. Finally, even the younger sons of the old nobility, either because of the custom of primogeniture or because of the impoverishment of their families, had to procure lands as a means of livelihood.

While individual entrants into this class had particular reasons for wanting to become landowners, the principal reasons, applicable to the class as a whole, were the availability of land on the market because of the spreading disintegration of the manorial system and the steadily increasing number of investors interested in acquiring land.

The breakup of the manorial system has been studied in the first chapter, and we saw that the main cause for this was the readiness on the part of many nobles to divest themselves of portions of their manors by sale or lease either to acquire money more readily or to avoid the losses from having to operate their estates in the face of labor shortage and shrinking profits. The increase in the number of investors resulted from certain economic and political factors which occurred in the second century of the Renaissance period. In transalpine Europe, in consequence of the economic revival after the Hundred Years' War, many merchants came into possession of more capital than they wished to reinvest in their business and some of them used the surplus to buy or lease land. Simultaneously, with the rise of the New Monarchies, the number of better paid officials and of wealthier professionals increased, and many of these were saving enough money to have surpluses for investment. In Italy, the faltering revival of the economy in the last century of the Renaissance discouraged investment in business enterprises, and so businessmen who still had some capital, safeguarded it by investing in land.[38] While many of these merchants and professionals never moved to the land but leased it out, some took on farming as a second interest, and others actually gave up their former vocations and became more or less substantial gentlemen farmers. The result was an increase in the number of gentry.

How great was the increase is impossible to ascertain, as only a few statistical studies are available, and even these are regional and, because of the nature of the source material, of questionable reliability. According to one of these studies,[39] the increase in Hainaut appears to have been about 200 per cent, but that included the nobility. Whereas in 1474 the two classes comprised only 6.4 per cent of the population, in 1502 they constituted 8.6 per cent, and in 1564–1573, 13.8 per cent. What part of this increase was due to the rise of the gentry alone is not known, but perhaps most of it, as the old nobility at no time constituted such a high percentage of the total population. But while the figures give some idea of the growth of the gentry class in one region of Belgium, obviously they cannot be used to define the increase in Europe as a whole. At best they can only be suggestive.

GENERAL TRAITS OF THE CLASS What characterized this class, at least before it succumbed to "squirearchism," was just this spirit of enterprise. Economically this expressed itself in a constant drive for more land and for greater profits from the land. Hence they seized at every opportunity to add acre upon acre, and they raised rents, enclosed fields, tried growing new crops, and introduced improved techniques into farming and more shrewdness into marketing. Socially this expressed itself in an equally constant drive for status, some of its members hoping thereby to preserve for themselves the pre-eminence which once their forbears enjoyed and others seeking to put as much distance between themselves and the commonalty socially as already separated them economically. Hence they scrambled for government positions and for advantageous marriages; they prepared their pedigrees and importuned for coats-of-arms; they sought culture by studying handbooks on etiquette, by conning chivalric literature, and by showing some interest in humanism; they sent their sons to colleges; they built impressive residences and surrounded themselves with servants; and they indulged in aristocratic diversions, in hunting, hawking, cardplaying, and even in jousting. In general, one gets the impression that it was a class which knew what it wanted and which extended itself to attain its objectives.[40]

PASTONS AS AN ILLUSTRATION To add some realism to this generalized view of the gentry we might examine the life of at least one specific family which belonged to this class, the Pastons of Norfolk County, England, for example. They left a rich collection of private letters which are highly revealing of their activities, interests, and manner of life, and of their shifting fortunes in consequence of their involvement in the hazardous Yorkist-Lancastrian feud. With the aid of similar private papers of some other contemporary families — *The Cely Papers* and *The Stonor Letters and Papers* — we can get a fairly authentic picture of their life.[41]

Although the Pastons claimed to be descendants of a Norman ancestor, they probably had a more plebeian origin, since one of the founders of the family's fortunes, Clement, was known to his fifteenth-century contemporaries as a "plain husbandman" and as a spouse of a bondwoman. However, although he may have been of peasant stock, Clement was no lowly rustic, as he already farmed more than 100 acres of land and had the vision and the means to send his son William to London to study law. William, reputed as "a right cunning man in law," secured first a sergeant's office in the Court of Common Pleas (1421) and then, in 1429, a judgeship worth 110 marks a year. Good at law, he was also very successful as an estate-builder, for he added manors by marrying a land-rich heiress and by purchase, and accumulated considerable bullion and plate (he is reported to have had £1,460 in gold in London and another £958 at Norwich priory, and 24 pounds, 11 ounces of gilt and 92 pounds, 2 ounces of ungilt plate). Then, to secure the future of the family, he negotiated a profitable marriage for his son John, and prepared him for the task of managing and safeguarding the estate. John measured up to his father's expectations: he warded off attacks on his inheritance from rival claimants — this was the period of the Wars of the Roses and so of strong-arm methods — and in addition, as a result of ingratiating himself with the knight Sir John Fastolf, secured the latter's property including a fine, new, thirty-room castle, as a bequest. The windfall, however, multiplied John's enemies, some of whom were of noble rank with "connections" at the royal court and so in a position to harass him with endless legal contests and with repeated forceful entries and trespasses. In the end, although John managed to hold his own, the struggle sapped his health and he died in 1466 "prematurely worn out." On John's death, much of his inheritance from Fastolf was taken away from his heir, also named John, but identified as Sir John as knighthood had been conferred on him by Edward IV in 1463. As frequently happened with third- and fourth-generation gentry, Sir John was more interested in London life and in soldiering than in managing his country estates. The result was a further depletion of the estate, much to the alarm of his mother who threatened to reduce his inheritance from her by twice the amount that he let slip through his hands. However, the family survived the travails; in fact, from the day of Sir John what it may have lost in substance, it gained in prominence. Sir John on one occasion served as Edward IV's champion, and his brother who succeeded him served as High Sheriff of Norfolk and was knighted by Henry VII at the battle of Stoke (1487). Thereafter the family tended to move in the lower ranks of the aristocracy rather than as gentry, and so we may terminate their history at this point.

Brief as the account is, it confirms the history and the general traits of the class as described above. And all that we need to do here to make the picture more complete is to say a few words about the living standards of the family when it was still in its gentry status.

The manor house of the Pastons must have been a modest one, for they added improvements as these came into use. John Paston, for example, wanted three chimneys added to his house at Mauteby. Until then the Pastons must have tolerated smoke in their halls. The building contained a hall, a master bedroom, perhaps another sleeping room or two, and a kitchen. Their furniture was simple. In the hall they had a long trestle table, and a small one also, a bench or two with tapestries to cover them, equipment for the fireplace, and two or three candle stands. Means permitting, there might have been a tapestry or some woven cloth to dress a wall or two, and a chair for the mistress, since chairs were not common except in the homes of the rich. The principal bedroom may have been more attractively furnished, perhaps even with a canopied bed with colored side curtains and rich coverlets and with a wall-hanging or two. If the family had household servants, there probably was a mattress or a trundle bed at the foot for the personal attendant, otherwise these would be used by the youngsters if there were insufficient bedrooms to accommodate them. There certainly was a chest for storing clothes and valuables including deeds, account books, and savings. On the chest, if there were no table, there may have been a basin and a ewer. There also was a fireplace with the necessary equipment, a bench, and a candle stand or two. The kitchen, unless the family was wealthy enough to afford separate structures, included the larder, pantry, and buttery — the Pastons combined their brewhouse and pantry under one roof. Naturally it too had a fireplace, an oven, and the needed utensils. At Hellesdon the Paston kitchen had two spits, one gridiron, two iron rakes, two pothooks, three brass pots, four great and one small basin, a storage pan for meat, twenty-four (?) pewter vessels, a dressing knife, two brendlets, one marble mortar and pestle. In the buttery they had six tablecloths, six towels, twelve napkins, six laten candlesticks, one silver plate, twelve silver spoons, two silver and two pewter salts, two pantry knives, twelve ale stands, two pewter basins with pitchers, one barrel of vinegar, and one barrel of verjuice.

This brief account reveals a rather modest if substantial way of life. There are indications of a receptiveness to improvements in material comforts, and even a few signs of oncoming pretentiousness. In general, however, the depiction is suggestive of a family that still has much social climbing to do before it can devote itself to high living and indolent squirearchism.

DECLINE Great as was this class in numbers and in influence, generally as supporters of strong central governments, it lost some of its ascendancy toward the close of the seventeenth century. It wasted too much of its resources in social climbing and in emulating the nobles, and since there was no second round of lucrative developments in husbandry to enable the class to meet this extra drain on its income — at least not until the agricultural "revolution" of the eighteenth century — the class fell behind economically, lost its drive, and succumbed to the role of genteel squires, so well depicted by Addison in his *Sir Roger de Coverley Papers*. Richelieu mocked those of France as "the indigent gentlemen." Only those of Spain, the proud *hidalgos,* sustained by the crown as they were, retained their influence.

Aristocracy

COMPOSITION AND PROMINENCE The highest class was the aristocracy. It consisted of three or four groups: the old noble families, the newly ennobled lines, the merchant princes, and the military princes. Of the old noble families many had become extinct through wars and the executioner's block as in England, or through impoverishment as on the continent, particularly in Germany; but there were still, in the

Renaissance days, a great number of families who traced their noble ancestry for several centuries and who lived and conducted themselves like their forbears. The attitude of a Montmorency, for example, who in 1560 came to the royal council of Fontainebleau with an escort of 800 horsemen, could not have differed much from that of a medieval magnate. Indeed, even such a "modern" state as Genoa had a goodly number of such nobles, one of which, the lordly Fieschi, could raise 4,000 men and fight for or against their government as their interests dictated.[42] The new compeers of this ancient nobility gained their ennoblement from the crown as compensation for faithful services rendered. This is particularly true in England where the Tudors more than doubled the number of nobles, as they raised the number of those sitting in the House of Lords from twenty-nine in Henry VII's day to sixty by the end of Elizabeth's reign; but it was also true, if to a lesser extent, on the continent. The merchant and military princes, men like the Centurioni of Genoa, Sforza of Milan, Fuggers of Germany, Canynges of Bristol, and Boleyns of London, secured admission to the aristocracy through their gold or their military achievements.

The aristocracy was still a very influential political force in the Renaissance period. It is true that it was losing its position at the council table and on the battlefield; that the bourgeois class and the monarchy had encroached upon its role in central and local government; and that the commoners, serving as the national host, began to be marshalled on the battlefields as important supplements to the knightly fighting arm. But it should be pointed out also that there were developments which promoted the position of the aristocracy, and that this occurred in all the countries of western Europe.

In Italy, many a commune of the medieval period gradually gave place to a despotism under a princely house or military general, and so the palazzo of its prince despot displaced the town hall as the focus of political and social life in town; and communes which did not succumb to princely despotism but instead became transformed into merchant republics by the end of the Middle Ages, as in the case of Genoa and Venice, witnessed the formation of a merchant aristocratic caste during the Renaissance, and then made the class exclusive by enacting laws prohibiting further admissions.[43] In Spain, after Ferdinand and Isabella implemented their program of centralization of authority, the days of the proud communes were over; and when the revolts of the *communeros* in Castile (1504–1521) and of the *germania* in Valencia (1521–1522) were suppressed, they ended in a victory not only for Charles I and for royalism but also for the proud *hidalgos,* who soon succeeded in monopolizing municipal offices and so rendered themselves both necessary and impregnable. Moreover, the privileges which distinguished them from the commoners in the Middle Ages were still theirs to enjoy throughout the Renaissance period. Thus, the law recognized that they were not to be burdened with taxes normally paid by the commoners; that they could not be drafted for military service, but only invited to serve; that they could not be imprisoned for debts except for those to the crown; that their houses, clothing, arms, and horses and mules were to be exempted from distraint in civil suits; and several other distinguishing exemptions.[44] In France, also, the old privileges of "gentillesse," similar to those enjoyed by the Spanish *hidalgos,* continued to preserve the class. Louis XI may have had a design of sinking the nobility in the merchant class, for he showed undue predilection for the estate of the "good merchants" and actually pursued a policy of encouraging the nobles to enter into business.[45] But since his inducement consisted of a promise that in undertaking an occupation which heretofore was considered beneath their dignities the nobles would suffer no derogation in honor, his design would not have really eliminated the nobility, though it might have reduced their parasitism. His successors, Francis I and Henry III, patronized the class no end, and definitely proclaimed its primacy and indispensability. Francis, for example, referred to himself as "the first gentleman" of his kingdom, and Henry stated explicitly that the strength of the crown rested principally on the nobility whose decline would weaken the state. Moreover, they increased the number of nobles by creating twenty-eight new peerages and fifty-five lesser titles, and Henry actually undertook to preserve the prestige of the class by agreeing to the request of his Estates that acquisition of a noble fief by a commoner should not qualify the purchaser for ennoblement.[46] In Germany, though many of the lesser nobility were brought to distress and even to extinction by the Renaissance economic forces, many of the more vigorous old houses increased their independence and influence from the thirteenth century on as a result of the decline of the imperial power following the collapse of the Hohen-staufen dynasty after 1250. In Poland the nobility was strong enough to transform the state into an aristocratic republic with the monarch as a figurehead. Finally, in all the lands there were men, a great number of them, who started out in the king's service as mere bourgeois and ended up as knights and lords. Balancing the two sides of the picture, we have to affirm that the nobility was still prominent during the Renaissance age. If the class was losing its monopoly in the field of government and war, the loss was not great enough to reduce it to impotence as sometimes assumed. The class cannot be dismissed as a negligible force, either in influence or in numbers.

This prominence, which the aristocracy still maintained in politics and in war, it bolstered by preserving its social pre-eminence. It did this by indulging in high and fashionable living, by elevating personal grace and social propriety into a cult, and by patronizing culture. Even though the motivation behind these may not always have been the safeguarding of this pre-eminence but was rather habit or simply love of high living and fine culture, the result nevertheless was just that. Extravagant living may be indulged in for the sake of pleasure, but it certainly helps to distinguish the devotee of this style of living from the commoners; and insistence on social protocol may be the natural result of appropriate upbringing, but it leads to ceremoniousness which becomes forbidding to the uninitiated. Hence whatever the motive, the result of aristocracy's way of life during the Renaissance was the preservation of its prominence.

It would, of course, be incorrect to assume that these practices originated with the Renaissance; for they began in the Middle Ages with the rise of chivalry and its concomitants — courtly literature and courtly love — with their emphasis on propriety, elegance, grace, and *amour*. But while recognizing their pre-Renaissance origins, we must admit that these habits were cultivated more intensively and intentionally during the Renaissance. The appearance of the new genre of court poetry, the *rhétoriqueur* type, and of numerous handbooks on the rules of knighthood and on the art of being a gentleman — Marshal Boucicaut's (Jean le Meingre's) *Livre des faits* in the fourteenth century, Caxton's translation of Jacques le Grand's *Book of Good Manners* and A. de La Sale's *Le Petit Jehan de Saintré* in the fifteenth century, and Baldassare Castiglione's *The Courtier* and Giovanni della Casa's *Galateo* in the following century — suggests this intensification and deliberateness. It is noteworthy that Castiglione's professed motive for the depiction of qualities deemed proper for a courtier was "to reject many silly fellows, who through presumption and ineptitude hope to acquire the name."

STANDARD OF LIVING The high style of living of the Renaissance aristocracy is revealed in their residences, furnishings, dress, and food.[47] For homes they were erecting palaces and villas in Italy, mostly of classic design, Italianate halls in England, and chateaux in France. Built for display and for ceremonious living, these residences were grand, multiple-chambered, stone edifices two or three stories high looking down upon enclosed courtyards artistically landscaped. Their interiors, with their paneled walls, coved ceilings, and grand staircases, were richly decorated and emblazoned with family emblems; and their furnishings, with the massive, carved furniture, luxurious rugs and tapestries, brilliant works of art, and ornamental silverplate and pewter, were as impressive as they were costly. The dress, for men as well as for women, was of the richest materials, silk, goldcloth, velvets, brocades, and laces. Here, for example, is how Matarazzo, an Italian chronicler, describes the dress which the Baglioni of Perguia wore at their son's wedding:

> Now His Highness Messer Astorre was clothed in gold from head to foot, and he had a very great number of robes and many fashions and patterns all of cloth of gold, and he had a collar very precious of massive gold which had been given to him by my Lords of Venice. And moreover his wife had all her garments of gold work, and the sleeves silk embroidered with precious pearls, and likewise her head was all covered with pearls; and His Highness Guido Baglione, his father, had a cloak worked with pearls and gold which was worth much money.[48]

Made seemingly not for comfort but for ostentation, their styles were as exaggerated as their colors were deep and varied and as their component articles were numerous. An actor once mocked that "seven pedlars' shops . . . will scarce furnish" the lady, and that "a ship is sooner rigged by far, than a gentlewoman made ready."[49] Looking at such a portrait as that of Henry Howard, Earl of Surrey,[50] one would imagine that these costumes, with all their elaborateness, must have been as exacting on one's composure as they probably were on one's comfort. They certainly were exacting on one's purse. In just one year, in 1603–1604, the Earl of Northumberland spent £540 on clothing, an amount almost twice as large as the total salary of his sixty-six servants for the same year.[51]

For food the aristocracy had plentiful supplies of meats of domestic and wild animals and fowl, of sweetmeats, of nuts, of sauces, spices, and wines. Dining was equivalent to feasting, and banqueting was frequent, extravagant, and ceremonious. This high living is described with some bitterness by Honoré Bonet, prior of the Benedictine house at Salon and a pensioner in the court of Charles VI of France. Attributing the decline of true chivalric virtue to the luxurious habits of the gentlefolk, he cries out:

> You are a people, so I have learned, who live luxuriously; if you do not have white bread, mutton, beef, and pork, partridges, chickens, capons, kids, ducks, pheasants and fat hares, and if you do not have more to-morrow than to-day, you are in discomfort; and if you do not have your soft white bed for one night, you are exhausted; you must have a white shirt, or you are dead; and if you do not have fine wines, the feast is worthless.[52]

Entertainment in which this class engaged were in keeping with its other habits. Hunting and hawking were the favorite outside sports and were regarded as a monopoly of the class. Tournaments were frequently staged, for several days at a time; and jousting, still a knightly privilege, was indulged in, even in bourgeois Florence. Less pretentious forms of diversion were bowling and tennis; and the latter was apparently gaining in popularity as we are told by Antonio Scaino, author of the first handbook on tennis (*Trattato del giusco della pella,* 1558), that there were "more tennis players in Paris than drunkards in England." Inside games were dice, chess, and backgammon. Gambling was very common. Much of the time was spent in *affaires d'amour*, in polite and witty conversation, in listening to recitations from romantic literature, in playing on some musical instrument, and in composing lyrics and sonnets, often enough addressed to persons other than legitimate spouses.

This generalized picture of the life of the aristocratic class varied somewhat with the wealth and the rank of the individual family. Naturally, there was a difference between the grand and gracious life of the court society and the less sophisticated habits of the provincial aristocracy. But, since the more lordly houses in the country emulated the standards of the society at the royal court, and the *petite noblesse* aped the ways of the higher nobility, the resulting standard of all was both high and pretentious. This fact appears quite clearly from the sixteenth-century journal of Sire de Gouberville et du Mesnil-au-Val, a *gentilhomme campagnard* of the Cotentin, Normandy. In an unusually detailed and intimately personal journal from 1549 to 1562 the good Sire included descriptions of stout manor houses, numerous and dutiful household staffs, plenteous boards, luxurious wardrobes, high banqueting, magnificent stag hunts, and ancient privileges taken for granted.[53] Except for the manor houses which had not yet yielded their simple amplitude to the extravagance and display demanded by Renaissance fashion, this is a picture of a standard of living which could be surpassed in pomp and vanities but not much in substance.

COMPARISON WITH MEDIEVAL ARISTOCRACY With this picture of the aristocratic class of the Renaissance before us, we can now ascertain in what ways this class differed from the aristocracy of the Middle Ages.

One notable change was in the composition of the class. Whereas in the Middle Ages, as Dante points out in the fourth book of his *Convivio,* the ignoble rich were not readily admitted as social equals to those nobly born, now there was less opposition to this mixture of gold with blood. Machiavelli's words "Strip us naked, and we shall all be found alike. Dress us in their clothing, and they in ours, we shall appear noble, they ignoble — for poverty and riches make all the difference,"[54] even if uttered by a forward plebeian rebel and therefore quite partisan, reveal what the public thought about the role of money in elevating one into the ranks of nobility. There was a difference, too, in the function of the class. Generally speaking, medieval aristocracy was preoccupied with feudal administration and with feudal wars. But by the time of the Renaissance, the growth of municipalities and of monarchies had steadily reduced the role of feudalism as a system of government and had diminished private wars. Even if interstate and civil wars provided the nobles with military opportunities, yet relatively the aristocracy found its chief preoccupations limited,[55] and it gradually entered the service of the crown and turned to high social living as a form of preoccupation.

A more noticeable difference was in the literacy and in the social polish of the class. Medieval aristocracy, certainly the fighting aristocracy, can hardly be considered as literate. Many nobles did not know how to write. The literature which they enjoyed was written for them by professional poets and recited to them by professional singers. There were exceptions, it is true, such as William IX, Duke of Aquitaine, who composed lyrics about his amorous successes, and Marie de France, who wrote those entertaining *lais*, and Joinville, the biographer of Louis IX, and, as the late Professor Thompson has shown in his study, *The Literacy of the Laity in the Middle Ages*, the exceptions grew in number in the later Middle Ages; but, in general, medieval aristocracy did not aspire to proficiency in letters and music. On the other hand, the aristocracy of the Renaissance made it their business to be cultivated in these two fields. There were, of course, many aristocrats who were adverse to letters. Poggio Bracciolini, having come to England in quest of manuscripts and preferment, left the island in disgust because he found the English aristocracy "much more interested in their farms and their food than in the encouragement of learning."[56] Ascham, in his *Scholemaster*, complained that "commonly the young gentlemen of England, go so unwillinglee to schole and run so fast to the stable."[57] Marineo, the Italian humanist in Spain, reported to a friend of his that "the Spaniards with few exceptions have no dealings with the Muses."[58] Luther protested that the German princes and lords instead of trying to get an education spent "their time in pleasure — driving, drinking, and folly" and preoccupied themselves "with the weighty duties of the cellar, kitchen and bedchamber."[59] Vives in a dialogue prepared for classroom use wrote:

> How much wiser you are than the multitude of nobles who hope that they are going to be esteemed as better born in proportion as they are ignorant of the art of writing. But this is scarcely to be wondered at, since this conviction has taken hold of the stupid nobles that nothing is more mean or vile than to pursue knowledge in anything.[60]

But allowing for the indifference to letters on the part of some nobles, one has only to recall such names as Sir Philip Sidney, the Earl of Essex, Lorenzo de'Medici, Marguerite d'Augoulême, Beatrice of Este, Montaigne, and one will realize that many lay aristocrats who were leaders in society were also leaders in the field of literature. Moreover, there is evidence that from the beginning of the sixteenth century the number of youths of the noble class going to college increased.[61] What was true of literacy and musical interests was equally true of artistic interests. The sense of the aesthetic can hardly be said to have had a place in the mind of a medieval noble. On the other hand, the Renaissance aristocracy were great patrons of art. Whether it was their appreciation of beauty, or whether it was merely for ostentation that they patronized the great artists, the fact remains that the Renaissance aristocracy surrounded themselves with the finest in all fields of art. In sum, they were as anxious to be cultivated dilettantes as they were eager to become exemplars of gentility, just as Castiglione recommended in the *Courtier*.

DISTINCTIVENESS OF ITALIAN ARISTOCRACY This portrayal of aristocracy holds true for most of western and central Europe. But there was one land, Italy, whose aristocracy possessed some distinctive traits.

The reasons for the difference were two: lack of one central authority for all Italy which could control the aristocracy by force and attract it by policy; and the exclusion, at least in a number of cities, of the nobility from political office. Hence, divided into numerous autonomous and quasi-autonomous units, all of which were torn by violent competitions between classes and individual families for control of government, Italy was a hotbed of factionalism, intrigue, revolts, and blood baths. And for the most part it was the aristocracy that was involved in this turbulence, and this involvement left its impress on the class.

The impress was one of finesse, finesse in the art of playing the potentate, proud and polished; finesse in dissimulation, in plotting and carrying out a "beautiful" coup; finesse in the art of living luxuriously and elegantly; finesse in dress habits and in habits of speech. In sum, the aristocratic ways became an art with them, cultivated to the point that it was natural with them.

Because of the above two influences, this Italian aristocracy lived energetically and even violently, seldom timidly, for they even feared greatly. Driven by the desire to succeed, they despised failure as nothing more, especially in competition with personal enemies, and gambled life itself in pursuit of success. Proud and selfish, capable of the finest refinements and unheard-of cruelties, given to impressive public parades and to devilish secret intrigue, engaging one moment in polite discourse on love and in another giving vent to livid hate, sweet perfumed and reeking with blood, the Italian princely aristocracy was a class and a cult.[62] It was distinctive, and by this distinction it has become a symbol, to many people, of Renaissance individualism. It was well with the world that this kind of individualism was limited to a small number and for the most part to Italy alone.

Hierarchic Conception of Society

"By the great ordinance of God, between them [the commonalty] and the gentry there is a great gulf fixed" — such was the belief of the Renaissance society. Note that this gulf was recognized not merely as the result of that mysterious attribute called ancestry, nor as the result of the obvious contrast between the polish and elegance of the aristocracy and the boorishness of the low classes — for all societies recognize such distinctions — but that it was believed to have been prescribed by the Almighty himself.

Alain Chartier, writing his *Quadrilogue invective* (*ca.* 1422) as a stirring appeal to all Frenchmen to rise to the rescue of fair France from the English, called upon the estates to shake off their lethargy and defection and to assume the true roles and responsibilities assigned to them from on high. In his *L'Arbre des batailles,* a study on the abuse of force and on the need to bridle it with law and justice, Honoré Bonet proclaimed the various estates to be as necessary to the state as branches are to a tree. In Germany, among the various literary pieces referring to the divine origin of the estates, perhaps the most popular theme was that of the visit of the Lord to Adam and Eve. According to this version the Lord decided to visit the errant First Parents to see their children. When Eve learned of this prospective visit, she did her utmost to make the surroundings attractive and her children presentable. Those

that were comely she instructed in the proper graces and allowed them
to remain in the open; but the ungainly she hid away in the stove and
in the hay. When the Lord came and noticed the nice children and their
proper deportment, He blessed them and created for them the high
estates of princes, knights, and wealthy citizens. Pleased with the Lord's
gift to her pretty ones, Eve became hopeful that he might bless her
unfortunate children also. She therefore produced them from their
hiding places and presented them to the Lord. He could not help
laughing at their state. Nevertheless, out of pity for their misfortune, he
created the several low estates so that they too might find a means of
livelihood. A naive explanation of the origin of the estate, one might
be tempted to say; but the very *naïveté* is proof of its wide circulation
and popular acceptance. In England, the theme of the estates was a
frequent topic among writers from the time of Gower to that of Lyd-
gate, Caxton, Alexander Barclay, and others. And when Shakespeare
made Ulysses say "Take but degree away, untune that string, and hark,
what discord follows,"[63] he really summed up the general attitude of his
contemporaries, to wit, that the estates were natural and necessary, that
they had respective responsibilities, and that fulfillment of these responsibilities and adherence to one's estate were essential for the well-being of
all. Even in Italy, where the emphasis seemingly was on enterprising
accomplishment — *virtù* the Italians called it — rather than birth, precedence was still conceded to the nobility. Thus Matteo Palmieri in his
work, *On Civil Life,* writes:

> He who seeks fame in the ability of the past generations deprives him-
> self of honor and merit. A pitiable creature is he who lives on the
> reputation of his ancestors. A man who deserves honors should offer
> himself, not his genealogy — *though we ought always to prefer the
> nobility as long as their achievements are equally good* [italics
> added].[64]

In Florence, in the early years of the 1500's, the authorities went beyond
a mere declaration of the precedence of the nobility. When the primacy
of this class was endangered by "the reprehensible habit . . . of giving
large and excessive dowries [1,600 florins]" which drove the less wealthy
"citizens of old and noble families" into incompatible marriage "alliances
with persons of a rank and condition very dissimilar to their own," or

which induced "many worthy young men, through their desire of a large dowry" to take "daughters of men who [were] wealthy but of a class and rank far inferior to their own," the council rushed to their protection by passing a regulation prohibiting such excessive dowries.[65] Bourgeois Florence, it would appear, not only recognized the distinction between mere wealth and social rank, but actually enacted legislation to preserve the latter.

This conception of a divinely ordained hierarchy was, of course, thoroughly medieval. The Renaissance accepted it, but it further accentuated the gulf by emphasizing the difference between the gentility and literacy of the aristocracy and the boorishness and ignorance of the commoners. Again and again the humanists, often the spokesmen for the aristocracy, showed utter contempt for the masses with such phrases as *"gens illa pauper et inops,"* or *"plebs infida, mobilis et rerum novarum avida."*[66]

Yet the gulf, however broad, was passable. Hierarchies were there, but it was possible to move from the lowest class to the highest, and vice versa. The movement from the lowest to the middle class was considerable, for peasants were turning apprentices and moving upward through the status of artisans to that of masters, merchants, and aldermen. Merchants through their usefulness to the crown as dispensers of gold and as officials occasionally reached the noble class; some reached this status by investing their capital in estates, turning into gentlemen farmers, and through intermarriage with the neighboring gentry, after two or three generations, into *petite noblesse.* On the other hand, some of the nobles, facing impoverishment, entered into business or married into money and so lost themselves in the bourgeois class. Those unwilling or unable to enter business or unsuccessful in finding rich spouses sometimes turned to brigandage, as did many German knights, or actually dropped to the level of peasants only to be mocked as the "barefoot gentry."

Present in civilized societies at all times, and not uncommon in the Middle Ages, this movement reached considerable proportions in the Renaissance period, particularly in those regions of Europe where economic developments were most promising. It was probably because of this increase in hierarchical mobility and the threat that it posed to social stability that there were so many public pronouncements, from the pulpit and the press, on the divine and natural origins of social hierarchism and on man's obligation to live by it.

1. This is true of the two classics by Burckhardt and Symonds which have done so much to fashion our thinking about the Renaissance.
2. Quoted from Huizinga, *The Waning of the Middle Ages*, 51.
3. Sir John Fortescue, *The Governance of England,* ed. Charles Plummer (Oxford: Clarendon Press, 1885), 114.
4. Cf., for example, Jehan Masselin, *Journal des états généraux de France tenus a Tours in 1484 sous le règne de Charles VIII*, trans. A. Bernier in *Collection de documents inédits sur l'histoire de France* (Paris: Imprimerie Royale, 1835), 523.
5. Quoted from Abel Lefranc, *La vie quotidienne au temps de la renaissance* (Paris: Librairie Hachette, 1938), 208.
6. Quoted from Langland's *The Vision of Piers the Plowman*, Done into Modern English by W. W. Skeat (London: Chatto and Windus, 1931), 110.
7. Quoted from Hutton Webster, *Historical Selections* (New York: D. C. Heath and Co., 1929), 541.
8. *Ibid.,* 754.
9. Cited from G. G. Coulton, *The Medieval Village* (New York: Cambridge University Press, 1925), 22–23.
10. H. G. Koenigsberger, *op. cit.,* 9, 11.
11. Luca Landucci, *A Florentine Diary from 1450 to 1516,* trans. Alice de Rosen Jervis (New York: E. P. Dutton & Co., 1927), 38–39, 116, 225.
12. Cited from A. L. Rowse, *The England of Elizabeth* (New York; Macmillan Co., 1951), 72. Rowse cites other contemporary reports which speak of the prosperity of English peasants in the southern part of the country. The total picture appears to be too favorable.
13. Cited from F. M. Powicke, "The Economic Motive in Politics," *EcHR,* XVI (1946), 89.
14. Cited from Johannes Janssen, *History of the German People at the Close of the Middle Ages,* trans. M. A. Mitchell and A. M. Christie (2d ed.; St. Louis, Missouri: B. Herder, 1905), I, 347.
15. *Ibid.,* I, 345–6.
16. For additional examples of well-to-do peasants see Paul Raveau, *op. cit.,* 244–63, and Tawney, *The Agrarian Problem in the Sixteenth Century* (London: Longmans, Green and Co., 1912), 32–33, 64–65, 132–3.

17. Lefranc, *op. cit.*, 207.

18. *Ibid.*, 212–3; Bezard, *op. cit.*, 219–23.

19. Cf. Rowland's "Dr. Merryman," in M. St. Clare Byrne, *op. cit.*, 40–41.

20. M. St. Clare Byrne, *op. cit.*, 41.

21. Bezard, *op. cit.*, 231–2.

22. Quoted from M. St. Clare Byrne, *op. cit.*, 132–3.

23. For a full account of the material welfare of the peasantry in the Middle Ages see H. S. Bennett, *Life on the English Manor: A Study of Peasant Conditions, 1150–1400* (Cambridge: Cambridge University Press, 1937). For a summary treatment see Duby, *op. cit.*, II, 526–31.

24. Cf. J. Saltmarshe's review of W. G. Hoskins, *The Leicestershire Farmer in the Sixteenth Century* in *EcHR,* XIV (1944), 196–8.

25. Cf. *The Cambridge Medieval History,* VIII, 731ff.

26. See above, 8.

27. Cf. the statement of the French jurisconsult Loyseau: "Les viles personnes du menu peuple n'ont pas droit de se qualifier bourgeois. Aussi n'ont-ils part aux honneurs de la cité, ni voix aux assemblées, en quoi consiste la bourgeoisie" (Gaston Zeller, *Les institutions de la France au xvie siècle* [Paris: Presses universitaries de France, 1948], 37).

28. A very revealing account of this matter is to be found in Julian Cornwall, "English Country Towns in the Fifteen Twenties," *EcHR,* 2d series, XV (1962), 54–69, and in W. G. Hoskins, "An Elizabethan Provincial Town: Leicester," in *Studies in Social History. A Tribute to G. M. Trevelyan,* ed. J. H. Plumb (London: Longmans, Green and Co., 1955), 41–45.

29. For the increase in relief cases in Belgium see M. Charles Verlinden, "Crises économiques et sociales en Belgique a l'époque de Charles quint," *Charles-Quint et son temps,* 177–90.

30. Cited from Janssen, *op. cit.*, II, 30. Janssen provides other examples of "strikes," but his picture of the artisan class is too favorable, to say the least.

31. J. U. Nichols, trans. *The Complete Works of François Villon* (rev. ed.; New York: Covici, Friede, 1931), 81.

32. On April 29, 1525, the Parlement in Paris reported "qu'il y a une grande quantité de femme indigentes qui couchet dans les rues avec leurs enfants" (Marcel Pöete, *Une vie de cité Paris de sa naissance a nos jours* [Paris: Auguste Picard, 1927], II, 324).

33. For a fuller treatment of the growth of this class consult Edward Potts Cheyney, *The Dawn of a New Era, 1250–1453* (New York: Harper & Brothers Publishers, 1936), the chapter on "The Rise of the Middle Class."

34. As to Toulouse, see Wolff, *op. cit.*, 537–97.

35. For a more detailed description of the residences and their furnishings, of food and dress of the middle class, see Sylvia Thrupp, *The Merchant Class of Medieval London (1300–1500)* (Chicago: University of Chicago Press, 1948), 131–5, and Lefranc, *op. cit.*, 137–41, 144–5, 147–53.

36. Based on Heers, *Le livre . . . de Giovanni Piccamiglio . . .*, 29–45.

37. For a critical study of the gentry in England see R. Trevor-Roper, *The Gentry 1540–1640, The Economic History Review Supplements,* no. 1, and Alan Simpson, *The Wealth of the Gentry, 1540–1660* (Chicago: University of Chicago Press, 1961). For France, consult Boutruche, *op. cit.*, 362–76, and Andre Viala, *Le parlement de Toulouse et l'administration royale laique, 1420–1525 environ* (Albi: Imprimarie-Reliure Orphelins-Apprentis, 1953), I, 260–87. For Italy see Luigi Simeoni, *Le Signorie, 1313–1559* (Milan: F. Vallardi, 1950), I, 372–89, and David L. Hicks, "Sienese Society in the Renaissance," *Comparative Studies in Society and History,* II (1960), 411–22.

38. Hicks, *op. cit.*, 416–9.

39. Koenigsberger, *op. cit.*

40. An excellent treatment of the ascent of one member of this class is Simpson's study of Nicholas Bacon, a yeoman's son who went into law and, through proper "connections" at the Tudor court, got important government posts and built a great estate (*op. cit.*, 22–114). For the social habits and ideals of this class see Arthur B. Ferguson, *The Indian Summer of English Chivalry. Studies in the Decline and Transformation of Chivalric Idealism* (Durham, North Carolina: Duke University Press, 1960).

41. This brief account is based largely on H. S. Bennett's delightful study, *The Pastons and Their England* (Cambridge: Cambridge University Press, 1951), and on Paul Murray Kendall's *The Yorkist Age: Daily Life during the Wars of the Roses* (New York: W. W. Norton & Company, Inc., 1962).

42. See Heers, *Gênes au xv*e *siècle,* 532–3.

43. On the hardening of Venetian aristocracy during the Renaissance see James C. Davis, *The Decline of the Venetian Nobility as a Ruling Class,* vol. LXXX of *The Johns Hopkins University Studies in Historical and Political Science* (Baltimore, Maryland: The Johns Hopkins Press, 1962), 15–38. In Genoa, breaking into the old-line nobility was difficult throughout the Renaissance period, but not into the merchant aristocracy, which became restrictive only toward the end of the period (*ibid.*, 20, and Heers, *Gênes au xv*e *siècle,* 561–2).

44. R. Trevor Davies, *The Golden Century of Spain, 1501–1621* (London: Macmillan and Co., Ltd., 1937), 53, 60–61. Very valuable evidence in Caroline B. Bourland's study of an actual court case concerning the status of two *hidalgos* (*The Case of Sancho de Almazan and Juan de la Camara versus the Crown of Castile and the Town Council of Arenas, 1514,* vol. XXIX of *Smith College Studies in History* [Northampton, Massachusetts: Smith College, 1947]).

45. On this policy see Gaston Zeller, "Louis XI et la merchandise," *Annales-economies, sociétés, civilizations,* I (1946), 331–41.

46. On the high place of aristocracy in France see G. Zeller, *Les institutions de la France au xvie siècle,* 12–20, and J. Russell Major, *Representative Institutions in Renaissance France, 1421–1559* (Madison: University of Wisconsin Press, 1960), 10–15.

47. An excellent treatment of the aristocratic way of life is to be found in W. L. Wiley's *The Gentleman of Renaissance France* (Cambridge: Harvard University Press, 1954).

48. Francesco Matarazzo, *Chronicles of the City of Perugia, 1492–1503,* trans. Edward Strachan Morgan (New York: E. P. Dutton and Co., 1905), 101.

49. Quoted from L. F. Salzman, *England in Tudor Times* (London: B. T. Batsford Ltd., 1926), 92.

50. See H. D. Trail and J. S. Mann (eds.) *op. cit.,* III, 213.

51. Gordon R. Batho, *op. cit.,* 445–7.

52. Translation taken from Lincoln Kilgour, *The Decline of Chivalry as Shown in the French Literature of the Late Middle Ages,* vol. XII of *Harvard Studies in Romance Languages* (Cambridge: Harvard University Press, 1937), 172, n. 1. For additional information on gentlefolk's food see William Harrison, *op. cit.,* 287; also "Wild Darrell's Diet at Warnick Lane from 16 April to 14 July, 1589," in Hubert Hall, *Society in the Elizabethan Age* (London: Swan Sonnenschein and Co., Ltd., 1902), Appendix, 212–33.

53. Of the several studies made of this journal the most delightful one is Katherine Fedden's *Manor Life in Old France. From the Journal of the Sire de Gouberville for the Years 1549–1562* (New York: Columbia University Press, 1933). The journal itself is published in two parts in the *Mémoires de la société des antiquaries de Normandie* for the years 1893 and 1895.

54. Machiavelli, *The History of Florence* (New York: The Colonial Press, 1901), bk. iii, ch. 4.

55. The decline of the political and military functions of the nobles in Italy is excellently treated by Anna T. Sheedy in chapter 4 of her book,

Bartolus on Social Conditions in the Fourteenth Century, vol. CDXIV of *Studies in History, Economics and Public Law* (New York: Columbia University Press, 1942).

56. Leonard E. Elliot-Binns, *England and the New Learning* (London: The Lutterworth Press, 1937), 28.

57. W. A. Wright's edition, 198.

58. Caro Lynn, *A College Professor of the Renaissance* (Chicago: University of Chicago Press, 1937), 186.

59. From his "Letter to the Mayors and Aldermen of All the Cities of Germany in Behalf of Christian Schools" in F. V. Painter, *Luther on Education* (Philadelphia: Lutheran Publication Society, 1889), 196.

60. Foster Watson, *Tudor School-Boy Life, The Dialogues of Juan Louis Vives* (London: J. M. Dent & Co., 1908), 69. Cf. also 44–45, 67, 173, 231. For actual examples of illiteracy on the part of Renaissance nobles see J. W. Thompson, *The Literacy of the Laity in the Middle Ages,* vol. IX of *University of California Publications in Education* (Berkeley: 1939), 196–7.

61. J. H. Hexter, "The Education of the Aristocracy in the Renaissance," *The Journal of Modern History,* XXII (1950), 1–20.

62. The spirit of this society is captured intimately in Jean Lucas-Dubreton, *La renaissance italienne. La vie et les moeurs (xve siècle)* (Paris: Amiot-Dumont, 1953).

63. *The Tragedy of Troilus and Cressida,* ed. N. Burton Paradise (New Haven: Yale University Press, 1927), Act I, sc. 3, verses 109–10.

64. Quoted from Hans Baron, "Background of the Florentine Renaissance," *History,* XXII (1937–38), 318.

65. Luca Landucci, *op. cit.,* 244, n. 1.

66. The subject of social hierarchism is treated by Ruth Mohl in her book, *The Three Estates in Medieval and Renaissance Literature* ("Columbia University Studies in English and Comparative Literature"; New York: Columbia University Press, 1933). See also Sylvia Thrupp's chapter "Trade and Gentility," *op. cit.,* 234–47.

Conclusion

By way of conclusion we may ask ourselves the question what does our survey of Renaissance economy and society reveal as to the innovations and as to the extent of deviation from the economy and society of the Middle Ages.

In agriculture the truly new development was the introduction of new crops; but some of these, like buckwheat, were only of marginal economic importance, and others, like maize and tobacco, appeared very late in the Renaissance period, so that the impact of either on Renaissance agriculture was really slight. Two other noticeable developments were the rise of market gardening and the increasing dissolution of the medieval manor. However, neither of these was an innovation in the strict sense of the term, as both were well advanced in the later Middle Ages. The difference was one of degree and not of kind; but even the degree of change was not as great as might be expected. Thus, for example, the European countryside during the Renaissance period was still covered with manors as functional units of agriculture even though on most of these manors in the western part of the continent tenants had replaced the medieval serfs. The change was in the legal status of the peasants, but as this change did not lead to any widespread enlargement of individual farms or to any improvement of farm operations, its effect on the agricultural economy was not substantial.

Commerce saw some promising innovations: trade with newly discovered transoceanic lands, the joint-stock company, the bourse, and double-entry bookkeeping. It also saw significant extension of some developments which originated in the Middle Ages — the regulated company, bills of exchange, insurance, and the shift to a system of permanent branch offices from the temporary quarters that were usually set up by the medieval merchants as they moved from fair to fair. Looked at with an eye to the future, all these developments were most promising. But viewed in relation to the Renaissance itself, they were certainly less significant; unless of course they were to be assessed in relation to the commerce of the early Middle Ages, when it was at its lowest. The real innovations came too late in the Renaissance period, and quantitatively their impact was not great enough before 1550 to effect an economic revolution. The other category of developments, namely, the extension of medieval practices, especially the universalization of the bills of exchange and the growth of regulated companies, had a considerable impact on Renaissance commerce, especially in promoting its international scope. But even this effect cannot be asserted absolutely if we recall that the volume of trade during the first century of the Renaissance period, that is, during the very time when this expansion was taking place, was below that of the medieval period, and that in the following century it was just attaining its pre-Renaissance levels. It is conceivable that the extension of these medieval economic institutions and practices during the Renaissance may have helped to mitigate the decline and then to promote the recovery, but one wonders how indispensable this extension was to the Renaissance economy if one compares the latter's condition with the steadily expanding economy of the two centuries prior to the Renaissance, that is, from about 1100 to 1325, when these institutions were still in their infancy. It would seem that the promise of greater things to come had to wait until the two categories, namely, the extension of the medieval instruments and the actual Renaissance innovations, came together in the first half of the sixteenth century, for it was after 1550 that the commercial revolution really developed.

As in commerce, so in industry some promising innovations appeared during the Renaissance. The factory system and the high-blast furnace were actual innovations, but both appeared late in the Renaissance period and were still quite rare by 1550. Their impact was therefore insignificant although their promise was great. Also appearing for the first time were some new industries, in particular, printing and the making of armaments. Printing spread very rapidly in the last century of the Renaissance, but except for a few places, Venice and Lyon especially, the printing establishments were relatively small, and so the impact of this industry on the economy as a whole was rather limited. The expansion of some medieval industries, such as the making of silk, glass, and brick, may have had a greater influence on the economy, but this influence did not reach significant proportions until after 1500, that is, toward the end of the Renaissance. Only the putting-out system, which was in operation at least since the 1200's, grew throughout the Renaissance and so exercised an increasing effect on economy by stimulating the growth of capitalism.

But two aspects of the industry, and these were of utmost importance, did not change. There was absolutely no change in the kind of power used to drive the machines, namely, water and wind power. Both were universally employed in the Middle Ages and both continued to be used throughout the Renaissance period; and as long as the source of power remained the same, no substantial transformation of industry could be expected. Nor was there any great change in the craft shop and the gild system of industrial organization. Although some gilds were disintegrating and others were turning into labor unions, the number of gilds actually multiplied, often under the patronage of state governments. One change that began to appear was the increasing subjection of the gilds to the state, but this had the effect of actually prolonging their life and hardening their structure.

On the whole, then, the sum total of changes in Renaissance industry did not add up to a transformation of the industry in the period.

In finance, the state bank, the creation of funded debts by the states, and the establishment of exchanges, like those in Antwerp, Lyon, and Geneva, were real innovations. Although they all had their roots in the Middle Ages, they expanded so greatly during the Renaissance that they may well be regarded as primarily a Renaissance development, and this phenomenal growth had a substantial impact on Renaissance economy after 1500. Still, it should be remembered that the principal suppliers of credit during the Renaissance period were the same as in the Middle Ages, namely, the money-changers, pawnbrokers, and the merchant bankers, and that the methods of state and municipal financing in these two periods were also quite similar. Naturally these continuations inhibited the invasion of innovations.

As to the role of the state in the economy of the Renaissance, the principle remained practically the same as in the Middle Ages. The state undertook to regulate various aspects of the economy either to protect the welfare of its citizens, to raise money for its needs, to promote industry, or to strengthen its diplomatic posture. The noticeable difference was that the Renaissance state, as its organization became more effective, increased its intervention. Only in the realm of finance was the effect of the Renaissance state truly substantial. The insatiable demands of the state for money stimulated the growth of exchanges, of credit financing, and of speculation, and these accelerated the development of capitalism.

There was no economic theory as such in the Renaissance period any more than in the Middle Ages. What ideas on the subject there were — occupational hierarchism, the notion of "just price," and the sinfulness of usury — were the same in both ages. And what departures from these ideas there were also were present in both periods. Only in one of these, in the matter of charging interest on loans, was there a change, as several prominent thinkers in the Renaissance period began to write openly in defense of charging interest, which fact would be indicative of a more tolerant attitude on the part of the Renaissance society toward the making of profit.

In society only one significant innovation appeared during the Renaissance period, that is, the rise of the gentry, a dynamic new class of landholders above the peasantry but below the nobility. In two matters, in the decrease in the number of serfs and in the cultural advancement of the aristocracy, the Renaissance period saw notable gains, but both movements had their origin in the Middle Ages and had attained sizable proportions by 1350. The middle class may have gained in influence after 1450, but it would be wrong to regard the Renaissance as a period dominated by this class, for the aristocracy continued to set the social and cultural standards in the Renaissance as it did in the Middle Ages and it still had a prominent role in state governments.

In sum, then, the Renaissance period was not an age of revolution in economy and society. Most of its innovations, and it had some full of promise for the future, did not appear early enough to affect the Renaissance radically. Unquestionably the best evidence of the absence of any phenomenal advancement is the fact that the first century of the Renaissance period was a period of economic decline and not of progress and that the second century was a period of recovery from the depression. Indeed, as a recent international conference held at the Sorbonne to discuss the problem of the supposed distinctiveness of the Renaissance reveals (*Actes du colloque sur la renaissance organisé par la Société d'histoire moderne — Sorbonne: 30 Juin-1er Juillet, 1956* [Paris: Librairie philosophique J. Vrin, 1958], 35–54), there are economic historians of great renown who doubt if even the sixteenth century was a century of decisive changes in Europe's economy.

Bibliography

The footnotes to each chapter include considerable bibliographical information. Much of this consists of specialized articles which need not be listed again. Here, therefore, only a select bibliography will be provided, with some French works included either because of their general coverage or because of the statistical and documentary information they include.

Some Aids

To keep abreast of what is being written on the economy of the Renaissance period, the student should scan the following journals for the numerous reviews and notices of new works appearing as well as for articles:

> *The Business History Review*
> *The Economic History Review*
> *The Journal of Economic History*
> *Journal of Economic and Business History*

For works which appeared in the past the student should consult the extensive bibliographies in *The Cambridge Economic History of Europe*. 3 vols. Cambridge: University Press, 1941–63.

Works Dealing with the Renaissance Economy in General

There are no recent works in English which deal with this subject specifically. The nearest approach is James Westfall Thompson's *An Economic and Social History of the Later Middle Ages*. New York: The Century Co., 1926, but the work is outdated. The best course, therefore, is to begin with some good economic histories of the Middle Ages, such as

Pirenne, Henri. *Economic and Social History of Medieval Europe*. New York: Harcourt, Brace and Co., 1937.
Luzzatto, Gino, *An Economic History of Italy from the Fall of the Roman Empire to the Beginning of the Sixteenth century*. Translated by Philip Jones. London: Routledge and Kegan Paul, 1961, and

The Cambridge Economic History of Europe already mentioned, and to follow these with such regional studies as,

Delumeau, Jean. *Vie économique et sociale de Rome dans le seconde moitié du xvie siècle. Bibliothéque des écoles françaises d'Athenes et de Rome.* No. 184. Paris, 1957.

Heers, Jacques. *Gênes au xve siècle. École pratique des hautes études* — VIe section. *Centre de recherches historiques, Affaires et gens d'affaires,* XXIV. Paris: S.E.V.P.E.N., 1961.

MacCaffrey, Wallace T. *Exeter, 1540–1640. The Growth of an English County Town.* Cambridge: Harvard University Press, 1958.

Raveau, P. *Essai sur la situation économique et l'état social en Poitou au xvie siècle.* Paris: Librairie des sciences politiques et sociales, 1931.

From there the student can turn to more specialized works on specific phases of the Renaissance economy.

Works Dealing with Agriculture

Bezard, Yvonne. *La vie rurale dans le sud de la région parisienne de 1450 à 1560.* Paris: Librairie de Paris, Firmin-Didot et cie, 1929.

Bloch, Marc. *Les caractères originaux de l'histoire rurale française.* Oslo: H. Aschehoug and Co., 1931.

Boutruche, Robert. *La crise d'une société. Seigneurs et paysans du Bordelais pendant la Guerre de Cents Ans.* Paris: Société d'éditions Les Belles Lettres, 1957.

Bowden, Peter J. *The Wool Trade in Tudor and Stuart England.* London: Macmillan and Co., Ltd., 1962 (contains valuable information on sheep raising).

The Cambridge Economic History of Europe. Vol. I, *The Agrarian Life of the Middle Ages.* Edited by J. H. Clapham and Eileen Power. Cambridge: The University Press, 1951.

Duby, Georges. *L'économie rurale et la vie des campagnes dans l'occident médiéval.* 2 vols. Paris: Aubier, Éditions Montaigne, 1962.

Orwin, Steward. *A History of English Farming.* London: Thomas Nelson and Sons, Ltd., 1949.

Raveau, Paul. *L'agriculture et les classes paysannes. La transformation de la propriété dans le haut Poitou au xvie siècle.* Paris: Librairie des sciences politiques et sociales, 1926.

Works Dealing with Commerce

Borel, Frédéric. *Les foires de Geneve au quinzieme siècle.* Geneva: H. Georg Librairie–Editeur, 1892.

Brésard, Marc. *Les foires de Lyon au xve et xvie siècles.* Paris: Auguste Picard, 1914.

Carus-Wilson, M. *Medieval Merchant Venturers.* London: Methuen and Co., Ltd., 1954.

Connell-Smith, Gordon. *Forerunners of Drake.* "Royal Empire Society Imperial Studies." London: Longmans, Green and Co., 1954.

Diffie, Bailey W. *Prelude to Empire. Portugal Overseas before Henry the Navigator.* Lincoln, Nebraska: University of Nebraska Press, 1960.

Gade, John Allyne. *The Hanseatic Control of Norwegian Commerce during the Late Middle Ages.* Leiden: E. J. Brill, 1951.

Gioffre, Domenico. *Gênes et les foires de change de Lyon à Besançon, École pratique des hautes études* — VIe section. *Centre de recherches historiques, Affaires et gens d'affaires,* XXI. Paris: S.E.V.P.E.N., 1960.

Heers, Jacques. *Le livre de comptes de Giovanni Piccamiglio, Homme d'affaires Génois, 1456–1459. École pratique des hautes études* — VIe section. *Centre de recherches historiques, Affaires et gens d'affaires,* XII. Paris: S.E.V.P.E.N., 1959.

Lapeyre, Henri. *Une famille de Marchands, les Ruiz.* Paris: Librairie Armand Colin, 1955.

Lopez, R. S. and Raymond, Irving W. *Medieval Trade in the Mediterranean World. Columbia University Records of Civilization, Sources and Studies,* No. 52. New York: Columbia University Press, 1955.

Mollat, M. *Le commerce maritime normand à la fin du moyen âge.* Paris: Librairie Plon, 1952.

Paragallo, Edward. *Origin and Evolution of Double Entry Bookkeeping.* New York: American Institute Publishing Co., 1938.

Penrose, Boies. *Travel and Discovery in the Renaissance, 1420–1620.* Cambridge: Harvard University Press, 1952.

Power, Eileen and Postan, M. M. (eds.). *Studies in English Trade in the Fifteenth Century.* London: George Routledge and Sons, Ltd., 1933.

Rambert, Gaston (ed.). *Histoire du commerce de Marseille.* 3 vols. Paris: Librairie Plon, 1949–57.

Roover, Raymond de. *L'évolution de la lettre de change, xive–xviiie siècles.* Paris: Librairie Armand Colin, 1953.

Ruddock, Alwyn A. *Italian Merchants and Shipping in Southampton, 1270–1600.* Southampton: University College, 1951.

Russell, J. C. *British Medieval Population.* Albuquerque, New Mexico: University of New Mexico Press, 1948.

Thrupp, Sylvia. *The Merchant Class of Medieval London (1300–1500).* Chicago: University of Chicago Press, 1948.

Ven Werveke, Hans. *Bruges et Anvers, huit siècles de commerce flammand.* Brussels: Éditions de la librairie encyclopedique, 1944.

Wolff, Philippe. *Commerce et marchands de Toulouse (vers. 1350–vers. 1450).* Paris: Librairie Plon, 1954.

Works Dealing with Industry

Lespinasse, Rene de. *Les métiers et corporations de la ville de Paris, xive–xviiie siècles.* 3 vols. Paris: Imprimerie nationale, 1886–1897.

Nef, John U. *The Rise of the British Coal Industry.* London: George Routledge and Sons, Ltd., 1932.

Salzman, L. F. *English Industries of the Middle Ages.* New ed. Oxford: The Clarendon Press, 1932.

Schubert, H. R. *History of the British Iron and Steel Industry from c. 450 B.C. to A.D. 1775.* London: Routledge and Kegan Paul, 1957.

Singer, Charles et al. *A History of Technology.* Vol. II, *The Mediterranean Civilizations and the Middle Ages.* Oxford: The Clarendon Press, 1956.

Unwin, G. *The Gilds and Companies of London.* Revised ed. London: George Allen, 1938.

White, Lynn Jr. *Medieval Technology and Social Change.* Oxford: The Clarendon Press, 1962.

Works Dealing with Finance

The Cambridge Economic History of Europe, III, 1963.

Ehrenberg, Richard. *Capital and Finance in the Age of the Renaissance, A Study of the Fuggers and Their Connections.* Translated by H. M. Lucas. New York: Harcourt, Brace and Co., 1928.

Roover, Raymond de. *Money, Banking, and Credit in Mediaeval Bruges.* Cambridge: The Mediaeval Academy of America, 1948.

Roover, Raymond de. *The Medici Bank. Its Organization, Management, Operations, and Decline.* New York: New York University Press, 1948.

Schick, Leon. *Une grand homme d'affaires au debut du xvie siècle — Jacob Fugger, École pratique des hautes études — VIe section. Centre de recherches historiques, Affaires et gens d'affaires,* XI. Paris: S.E.V.P.E.N., 1957.

Usher, Abbott Payson. *The Early History of Deposit Banking in Mediterranean Europe. Harvard Economic Studies,* Vol. LXXV. Cambridge: Harvard University Press, 1943.

Works Dealing with Economic Theory and with "Statism"

The Cambridge Economic History of Europe, III.

Cole, Charles Woolsey. *French Mercantilist Doctrines before Colbert.* New York: Richard R. Smith, Inc., 1931.

Heckscher, Eli F. *Mercantalism.* Translated by M. Shapiro and revised by E. F. Söderlund. New York: The Macmillan Co., 1955.

Noonan, John T., Jr. *The Scholastic Analysis of Usury.* Cambridge: Harvard University Press, 1957.

Rich, Edwin Ernest. *Merchant of the Staple of England*. Cambridge: University Press, 1937.

Tawney, R. H. *Religion and the Rise of Capitalism*. Baltimore: Penguin Books Limited, 1938.

Works on Society

Bennett, H. S. *The Pastons and their England*. Cambridge: University Press, 1951.

Cheyney, Edward Potts. *The Dawn of a New Era, 1250–1453*. New York: Harper & Brothers Publishers, 1936.

Davis, James C. *The Decline of the Venetian Nobility as a Ruling Class. The Johns Hopkins University Studies in Historical and Political Science*, Vol. LXXX. Baltimore, Maryland: Johns Hopkins Press, 1962.

Fedden, Katherine. *Manor Life in Old France. From the Journal of the Sire de Gouberville for the years 1549–1562*. New York: Columbia University Press, 1933.

Ferguson, Arthur B. *The Indian Summer of English Chivalry. Studies in the Decline and Transformation of Chivalric Idealism*. Durham, North Carolina: Duke University Press, 1960.

Huizinga, Johan. *The Waning of the Middle Ages*. Garden City, New York: Doubleday and Co., 1954.

Landucci, Luca. *A Florentine Diary from 1450 to 1516*. Translated by Alice de Rosen Jervis. New York: E. P. Dutton and Co., 1927.

Lefranc, Abel. *La vie quotidienne au temps de la renaissance*. Paris: Librairie Hachette, 1938.

Lucas-Dubreton, Jean. *Daily Life in Florence in the Time of the Medici*. Translated by A. Lytton Sells. London: George Allen and Unwin Ltd., 1960.

Major, J. Russell. *Representative Institutions in Renaissance France, 1421–1559*. Madison, Wisconsin: University of Wisconsin Press, 1960.

Mohl, Ruth. *The Three Estates in Medieval and Renaissance Literature. Columbia University Studies in English and Comparative Literature*. New York: Columbia University Press, 1933.

Rowse, A. L. *The England of Elizabeth*. New York: The Macmillan Co., 1951.

Simpson, Alan. *The Wealth of the Gentry, 1540–1660*. Chicago: University of Chicago Press, 1961.

Wiley, W. L. *The Gentleman of Renaissance France*. Cambridge: Harvard University Press, 1954.

Zeller, G. *Les institutions de la France au xvie siècle*. Paris: Presses Universitaires de France, 1948.

Index

Tennis, gaining in popularity, 146
Thurzo (mining firm), 86, 87
Tolls, profusion of, 104
Tours, silkmaking in, 62
Trade: international, 21, 25, 27, 72–73, 90; loss of, with China, 31; see also commerce

Usufacture, 63
Usury, 107–10

Venice: commerce of, 22, 23; decline of, 26; "state" shipping, 101

Viticulture, 3–4
Vives, on indifference of nobility to learning, 148

Water wheels, 60
Wimpfeling, on peasantry in Alsace, 126
Winchombe, John, cloth factory of, 68–69

Zaccharia, Benedetto (capitalist trader in alum), 44, 68, 71

ACKNOWLEDGMENTS

The author wishes to thank the following publishers for permission to quote from their publications listed below:

Edward Arnold (Publishers) Ltd. London, England	*The Waning of the Middle Ages* by Johan Huizinga
Ernest Benn Limited London, England	*Men and Manners of Old Florence* by T. Fisher Unwin
Cambridge University Press New York	*The Medieval Village* by G. G. Coulton
The Clarendon Press London, England	*The Works of Thomas Deloney* edited by F. O. Mann
Jonathan Cape Limited London, England	*Capital and Finance in the Age of the Renaissance* by Richard Ehrenberg
Chatto and Windus London, England	*The Vision of Piers the Plowman.* Done into Modern English by W. W. Skeat
J. M. Dent & Sons Ltd. Publishers London, England	*Tudor School-Boy Life* by Foster-Watson
E. P. Dutton & Co. Inc. New York	*A Florentine Diary from 1450 to 1516* by Luca Landucci
Harvard University Press Cambridge, Massachusetts	*Chronicles of the City of Perugia, 1492–1503* by Matarazzo
The Macmillan Company New York	*The England of Elizabeth* by A. L. Rowse
Methuen & Co. Ltd., Publishers London, England	*Elizabethan Life in Town and Country* by M. St. Clare Byrne
New York University Press New York	*The Medici Bank, Its Organization, Management, Operations, and Decline* by Raymond de Roover
Presses Universitaires de France Paris	*Les débuts de l'age moderne,* Vol. VIII of *Peuples et civilizations, histoire générale* by H. Hauser and A. Renaudet
The Viking Press Inc., Publishers New York	*The Portable Renaissance Reader,* edited by Bruce Ross and Mary Martin McLaughlin